CW00429550

Cyclists &
Walkers
Welcome

Information
at your fingertips

This pocket guide is aimed at cyclists and walkers looking for quality-rated accommodation along the way. You will find a selection of hotels, B&Bs, and self-catering holiday homes in England that actively encourage walking and cycling. Proprietors go out of their way to make special provisions for guests who enjoy these activities to ensure they have a comfortable stay.

Star ratings

Establishments are awarded a rating of one to five stars based on a combination of quality of facilities and services provided. The more stars, the higher the quality and the greater the range of facilities and level of service.

The process to arrive at a star rating is very thorough to ensure that when you book accommodation you can be confident it will meet your expectations. Enjoy England professional assessors visit establishments annually and work to strict criteria to rate the available facilities and service.

A quality score is awarded for every aspect of the experience. For hotels and B&B accommodation this includes the comfort of the bed, the quality of the breakfast and dinner and, most importantly, the cleanliness. For self-catering properties the assessors also take into consideration the layout and design of the accommodation, the ease of use of all appliances, the range and quality of the kitchen equipment, and the variety and presentation of the visitor information provided. The warmth of welcome and the level of care that each establishment offers its guests are noted, and places that go the extra mile to make every stay a special one will be rewarded with high scores for quality.

All the national assessing bodies (VisitBritain, VisitScotland, Visit Wales and the AA*) now operate to a common set of standards for rating each category of accommodation, giving holidaymakers and travellers a clear guide on exactly what to expect at each level. An explanation of the star ratings is given below:

Ratings made easy

★	Simple, practical, no frills
★★	Well presented and well run
★★★	Good level of quality and comfort
★★★★	Excellent standard throughout
★★★★★	Exceptional with a degree of luxury

For full details of Enjoy England's Quality assessment schemes go online at

enjoyengland.com/quality

Awaiting confirmation of rating

At the time of going to press some establishments featured in this guide had not yet been assessed for their rating for the year 2007 and so their new rating could not be included. Rating Applied For indicates this.

* The AA does not assess self-catering properties.

Gold and Silver Awards

The Enjoy England awards are highly prized by proprietors and are only given to hotels and bed and breakfast accommodation offering the highest level of quality within their star rating, particularly in areas of housekeeping, service and hospitality, bedrooms, bathrooms and food.

National Accessible Scheme

Establishments with a National Accessible Scheme rating provide access and facilities for guests with special visual, hearing and mobility needs.

Designators explained

Hotel	A minimum of six bedrooms, but more likely to have more than 20.
Small Hotel	A maximum of 20 bedrooms and likely to be more personally run.
Townhouse Hotel	In a city or town-centre location, high quality with a distinctive and individual style. Maximum of 50 bedrooms, with a high ratio of staff to guests. Possible no dinner served, but room service available. Might not have dining room, so breakfast may be served in bedrooms.
Guest Accommodation	Encompassing a wide range of establishments from one room B&Bs to larger properties which may offer dinner and hold an alcohol licence.
B&B	Accommodating no more than six people, the owners of these establishments welcome you into their own home as a special guest.
Guest House	Generally comprising more than three rooms. Dinner is unlikely to be available (if it is, it will need to be booked in advance). May be licensed.
Farmhouse	B&B, and sometimes dinner, but always on a farm.
Restaurant with Rooms	A licensed restaurant is the main business but there will be a small number of bedrooms, with all the facilities you would expect, and breakfast the following morning.
Inn	Pub with rooms, and many with restaurants, too.
Self Catering	Chose from cosy country cottages, smart town-centre apartments, seaside villas, grand country houses for large family gatherings, and even quirky conversions of windmills, railway carriages and lighthouses. Most take bookings by the week, generally from a Friday or Saturday, but short breaks are increasingly offered, particularly outside the main season.
Serviced apartments	City-centre serviced apartments are an excellent alternative to hotel accommodation, offering hotel services such as daily cleaning, room service, concierge and business centre services, but with a kitchen and lounge area that allow you to eat and relax when you chose. A telephone and internet access tend to be standard. Prices are generally based on the property, so they often represent excellent value for families and larger groups. Serviced apartments tend to accept bookings for any length of period, and many are operated by agencies whose in-depth knowledge and choice of properties makes searching easier at busy times.
Hostel	Safe, budget-priced, short-term accommodation for individuals and groups.

How to use this guide

Each accommodation entry contains information that proprietors provide regional tourist partners (except for ratings and awards).

① ② ③   ④ ⑤

BOWNESS-ON-WINDERMERE

Lindeth Howe Country House Hotel   ★★★Hotel
Lindeth Drive, Longtail Hill, Windermere, Cumbria, LA23 3JF   SILVER AWARD

T:	+44 (0) 1539 445759
E:	hotel@lindeth-howe.co.uk
W:	lindeth-howe.co.uk
Bedrooms:	26; sleeps 56
Prices:	Double: £200-£210 per room per night breakfast included
	Debit/credit card, euros accepted
Open:	Year round
Description:	Lindeth Howe Country House is a tranquil retreat situated one mile south of Bowness-on-Windermere. Set in six acres of stunning gardens, located on a hillside with spectacular views of Lake Windermere and the Fells beyond.
Facilities:	Rooms: 🛏️📺
	General: 🏠✕🅿️
	Leisure: 🚴‍♂️🐾

⑥ ⑦ ⑧   ⑨ ⑩

1	Postal town
2	Establishment name
3	Establishment address (or booking address if self catering)
4	Enjoy England Quality star rating and designator
5	Gold or Silver Award where applicable
6	Telephone, email and website address – note that web addresses are shown without the prefix www.
7	Accommodation details, prices and details of when establishment is open
8	At-a-glance facility symbols (for key see facing page)
9	Accessible rating where applicable
10	Cyclists/Walkers Welcome where applicable

Please note that sample entry is for illustration purposes only.
Not all symbols shown will apply to this establishment.

Key to symbols

Rooms/Units

- ⁜ Non-smoking rooms/units available
- 📻 Radio
- ☕ Tea/coffee facilities in all bedrooms
- 📞 Phone in all bedrooms
- 🛏 Cots available
- 🔥 Central heating
- 📺 Colour TV
- 📼 Video player
- 💽 DVD player
- 🛏 Four-poster bed available
- 🧊 Freezer
- 🫧 Dishwasher
- 💨 Hairdryer in all bedrooms
- ✍ Internet

General

- ✂ Non-smoking establishment
- ☽ Night porter
- P Parking on site
- ☎ Public phone
- ♨ Open fires
- 🧒 Children welcome (check with accommodation for minimum age)
- 🪑 Highchairs
- 🍸 Licensed bar
- 🚌 Coach parties welcome
- ✕ Restaurant
- 🛒 Shop on site
- 🎵 Evening entertainment
- ✿ Garden/patio
- 🐾 Pets welcome
- 🪑 Lounge
- 🖼 Linen provided
- 🏷 Linen available for hire
- 🧺 Washing machine or laundry facilities
- 🚿 Shower on site

Leisure

- 🏊 Swimming pool – outdoor
- 🏊 Swimming pool – indoor
- ∪ Riding/pony trekking nearby
- 🎾 Tennis court(s)
- ⚫ Games room
- 🎣 Fishing nearby
- ⛳ Golf nearby
- 🚲 Cycle hire nearby

Mobility Symbols

Typically suitable for a person with sufficient mobility to climb a flight of steps but who would benefit from fixtures and fittings to aid balance.

Typically suitable for a person with restricted walking ability and for those who may need to use a wheelchair some of the time and can negotiate a maximum of three steps.

Typically suitable for a person who depends on the use of a wheelchair and transfers to and from the wheelchair in a seated position. This person may be an independent traveller.

Typically suitable for a person who depends on the use of a wheelchair in a seated position. This person also requires personal/mechanical assistance to aid transfer (eg carer, hoist).

Visual Impairment Symbols

Typically provides key additional services and facilities to meet the needs of visually impaired guests.

Typically provides a higher level of additional services and facilities to meet the needs of visually impaired guests.

Hearing Impairment Symbols

Typically provides key additional services and facilities to meet the needs of guests with a hearing impairment.

Typically provides a higher level of additional services and facilities to meet the needs of guests with a hearing impairment.

Cyclists Welcome and Walkers Welcome

Participants actively encourage cycling and walking by providing clean up areas for washing or drying off, help with special meal arrangements, maps and books to look up for cycling and walking routes.

ASTON CLINTON

West Lodge Hotel ★★Hotel

45 London Road, Aston Clinton, Aylesbury, Buckinghamshire, HP22 5HL

T:	+44 (0)1296 630362
E:	jibwl@westlodge.co.uk
W:	westlodge.co.uk
Bedrooms:	15 • sleeps 21
Prices:	Double: £88; Single: £60 both per room per night breakfast included • Debit/credit card accepted
Open:	Year round except New Year
Description:	Elegance, quality and good service at our 19thC hotel. Enchanting English garden, spa room with sauna and Jacuzzi.
Facilities:	Rooms: 🛁📺📶 General: ⚡✕☼🍴

CHARTRIDGE

Chiltern Ridge B&B ♦♦♦♦Guest Accommodation

Old Sax Lane, Chartridge, Chesham, Buckinghamshire, HP5 2TB

T:	+44 (0)1494 785732
E:	chilternridge1@hotmail.com
Bedrooms:	1 • sleeps 2
Prices:	Double: £50 per room per night breakfast included Euros accepted
Open:	Year round
Description:	Luxurious, detached annexe in the middle of the countryside with easy access to M40, M25 and M1.
Facilities:	Rooms: 🔌✕🛁📺📶📶 General: ⚡P☼🍴 Leisure: ▶

ELY

Forty Farmhouse ★★★Self Catering

7 Lisle Lane, Ely, Cambridgeshire, CB7 4AS

T:	+44 (0)1353 615406
E:	fortyfarmhouse@aol.com
W:	tiscover.co.uk/gb/guide/5gb,en/objectId,ACC21574gb/home.html
Units:	1 • sleeps 1
Prices:	£420 per week year round
Open:	Year round
Description:	Three-bedroom, modern, traditional, terrace townhouse. Enclosed courtyard garden. Well placed for cathedral, river, market square and railway station.
Facilities:	General: P☼

BODMIN

Bedknobs B&B   ♦♦♦♦ Guest Accommodation

Polgwyn, Castle Street, Bodmin, Cornwall, PL31 2DX   SILVER AWARD

T:	+44 (0)1208 77553
E:	gill@bedknobs.co.uk
W:	bedknobs.co.uk
Bedrooms:	3 • sleeps 6
Prices:	Double: £25-£40 per person per night breakfast included Debit/credit card accepted
Open:	Year round
Description:	Cornwall Tourism Awards (CTA) 2005 – Sustainable Tourism Initiative of the Year – Silver Award; CTA 2004 – Guesthouse/B&B of the Year-Highly Commended; CTA 2003 – Guesthouse/B&B of the Year.
Facilities:	Rooms: ▥ General: ⚲ 🏳

BOSSINEY

Halgabron Mill Cottages   ★★★ Self Catering

St Nectan's Glen, Tintagel, Cornwall, PL34 0BB

T:	+44 (0)1840 779099
E:	robin@halgabronmill.co.uk
W:	halgabronmill.co.uk
Units:	4 • sleeps 13
Prices:	From £200-£664 per week • Debit/credit card accepted
Open:	Year round
Description:	Four stone cottages completely secluded in the heart of St Nectan's Glen. With old beams, lead latticed windows; wood-burning stoves and night storage heaters. There are walks through 22 acres of private gardens and woodland.
Facilities:	General: ✿

BUDE

Creathorne Farm B&B   ★★★★★ Farmhouse

The Granary, Creathorne Farm, Bude, Cornwall, EX23 0NE

T:	+44 (0)1288 361077
E:	alisonnicklen@tiscali.co.uk
W:	creathornefarm.co.uk
Bedrooms:	3 • sleeps 3
Prices:	Double: £25-£30 per person per night breakfast included Debit/credit card accepted
Open:	Year round
Description:	Luxury farm B&B approximately one mile from North Cornwall coastal path and renowned sandy surfing beach.
Facilities:	Rooms: ▥ General: ⚲✿🏳

BUDE

Kings Hill Meadow ★★★★★ Guest Accommodation
Bagbury Road, Bude, Cornwall, EX23 8SR   SILVER AWARD

T:	+44 (0)1288 355004
E:	kingshillmeadow@btinternet.com
W:	kingshillmeadow.co.uk
Bedrooms:	5 • sleeps 15
Prices:	Double: £27.50-£37.50 per person per night breakfast included • Debit/credit card accepted
Open:	Year round
Description:	A family-run B&B in a new property (completed August 2004) with five en suite bedrooms on the outskirts of Bude.
Facilities:	Leisure: ⚲🚴

BUDE

The Green House ♦♦♦♦ Guest Accommodation
16 Burn View, Bude, Cornwall, EX23 8BZ   SILVER AWARD

T:	+44 (0)1288 355587
Bedrooms:	3 • sleeps 8
Prices:	Double: £46-£56 per room per night breakfast included
Open:	Year round
Description:	Beautifully and sympathetically restored Victorian house in the centre of Bude, overlooking the golf course, walking distance to two Blue Flag beaches, shops and many good restaurants.
Facilities:	Rooms: ✕☀📺 General: ✕P Leisure: ▶

BUSVANNAH

Bay View ★★★ B&B
Busvannah, Penryn, Cornwall, TR10 9LQ

T:	+44 (0)1326 372644
E:	dawnemmerson@aol.com
W:	falmouth-bandb.co.uk
Bedrooms:	3 • sleeps 3
Prices:	Double: £20-£24 per person per night breakfast included Debit/credit card accepted
Open:	Year round
Description:	Bay View has stood at the top of Busvannah since 1880, with stunning views across fields to Falmouth Harbour from bedrooms. It is in a quiet, semi-rural location, but just two miles from the heart of Falmouth.
Facilities:	Rooms: General: ✕

CALLINGTON

Berrio Mill ★★★★ Self Catering

Golberdon, Callington, Cornwall PL17 7NL

T:	+44 (0)1579 363252
E:	enquiries@berriomill.co.uk
W:	berriomill.co.uk
Units:	2 • sleeps 6
Prices:	From £180 to £590 per week
Open:	Year round
Description:	Two new barn conversion cottages in beautiful location next to millstream and river, ideal for bird watching, fishing, walking and wildlife.
Facilities:	Leisure: ♪

FOUR CROSS

Sunnyside B&B ★★★★ B&B

Treluswell, Penryn, Cornwall, TR10 9AN

T:	+44 (0)1326 379254
E:	enquiries.sunnyside@btinternet.com
W:	sunnysidebedandbreakfast.co.uk
Bedrooms:	3 • sleeps 5
Prices:	Double and single rooms: £25-£27 per person per night breakfast included
Open:	Year round
Description:	Sunnyside is open all year round and is prominently situated on the outskirts of Falmouth and Penryn. Just about anywhere in Cornwall is within one hour's drive.
Facilities:	Rooms: ♦✕🖤🆑📺 General: ✁P❀ Leisure: ▶

LEEDSTOWN

Little Pengelly Self Catering rating applied for

Trenwheal, Leedstown, Hayle, Cornwall TR27 6BP

T:	+44 (0)1736 850452
E:	maxine@littlepengelly.co.uk
W:	littlepengelly.co.uk
Units:	2 • sleeps 2
Prices:	From £280-£420 per week
Open:	Year round
Description:	Peaceful, secluded, converted barn, mid peninsular. Spacious rooms. Double room, plus comfortable double sofa bed in lounge. Own patio and garden. Plentiful parking. Pets welcome.
Facilities:	General: P❀🐾🖳

MEVAGISSEY

Portmellon Cove ♦♦♦♦♦ Guest Accommodation

121 Portmellon Park, Mevagissey, Cornwall, PL26 6XD   SILVER AWARD

T:	+44 (0)1726 843410
Bedrooms:	3 • sleeps 6
Prices:	Double: £35-£45 per person per night breakfast included Debit/credit card, euros accepted
Open:	Year round
Description:	Quality, licensed guesthouse offering beautiful sea views from its luxurious bedrooms. Close to Mevagissey, Eden, Heligan and breathtaking coastal walks. Good pubs nearby.
Facilities:	Rooms: ᴮ✕✆🛏📺 General: ✕🛇♨🏴

MOUSEHOLE

Poldark Cottage ★★★ Self Catering

Booking: An Benolva, Fore Street, TR18 5JD

T: **W:**	+44 (0)1736 330609 cornwalltouristboard.co.uk/poldarkcottage
Units:	Sleeps 2-6
Prices:	From £175-£665 per week
Open:	Year round
Description:	Poldark Cottage is Grade II Listed Cornish Cottage, with three star rating, right next to the picturesque Mousehole Harbour, fully equipped for self-catering for two-six people. The main cottage has all the traditional features.
Facilities:	General: ✿

NORTH TAMERTON

Hill Cottage ★★★★ Self Catering

Booking: Beer Mill Farm, Clawton, EX22 6PF

T: **E:** **W:**	+44 (0)1409 253093 enquiries@selfcateringcottagesdevon.co.uk selfcateringcottagesdevon.co.uk
Units:	1 • sleeps 2
Prices:	From £120-£1,050 per week
Open:	Year round
Description:	An individual stone cottage, nestling in open countryside on the Devon/Cornwall border with views over the picturesque River Tamar. Hill Cottage stands alone in its own private, tiered garden with mature fruit trees and protective hedgerow.
Facilities:	General: ✿

PELYNT

Hendra Farm Cottages ★★★★ Self Catering

Pelynt, Looe, PL13 2LU

T:	+44 (0)1503 220701
E:	info@hendrafarmcottages.co.uk
W	hendrafarmcottages.co.uk
Units:	9 • sleeps 23
Prices:	From £165-£595 per week
Open:	Year round
Description:	Just four miles from the popular resort of Looe, Hendra Farm Cottages attract a wide range of holiday makers all year round.
Facilities:	General: ♣

PENZANCE

39 The Park ★★ Self Catering

Booking: 150 Kings Road, Bebington, CH63 8PZ

T:	+44 (0)151 608 1294
Units:	1 • sleeps 4
Prices:	From £200-£425 per week
Open:	Year round
Description:	Comfortable, relaxing and welcoming accommodation in the extensive mature gardens of an ancient Cornish Manor House.
Facilities:	Rooms: ☎ General: ♣ Leisure: ⚲

PENZANCE

Glencree House ♦♦♦ Guest Accommodation

2 Mennaye Road, Penzance, Cornwall, TR18 4NG

T:	+44 (0)1736 362026
E:	stay@glencreehouse.co.uk
W	glencreehouse.co.uk
Bedrooms:	8 • sleeps 14
Prices:	Double: £18-£32; Single: £20.50-£30; both per person per night breakfast included • Debit/credit card accepted
Open:	Year round
Description:	Victorian house in a peaceful location 50 yards from the seafront. Friendly and welcoming, with high standard of personal service. Bright, spacious rooms, mostly en suite and some with sea views, four-poster and kingsize available.
Facilities:	Rooms: ▥⟐ General: ✗⟐

11

PENZANCE

Mount Prospect Hotel ★★★Hotel
SILVER AWARD

Britons Hill, Penzance, Cornwall, TR18 3AE

T:	+44 (0)1736 363117
E:	enquiries@hotelpenzance.com
W:	hotelpenzance.com
Bedrooms:	27 • sleeps 50
Prices:	Double: £55-£66; Single: £65-£74; both per person per night breakfast included • Debit/credit card accepted
Open:	Year round
Description:	Cornwall Tourism Awards (CTA) 2005 – Hotel of the Year – Silver Award; CTA – Hotel of the Year – Highly Commended 2002/03/04; Restaurant of the Year – Finalist 2002 & 2004
Facilities:	Rooms: ▥ General: ◑✿⌘ Leisure: ⬎

PENZANCE

Tremont Hotel ◆◆◆◆Guest Accommodation

Alexandra Road, Penzance, Cornwall, TR18 4LZ

T:	+44 (0)1736 362614
E:	info@tremonthotel.co.uk
W:	tremonthotel.co.uk
Bedrooms:	9 • sleeps 15
Prices:	Double: £25-£28; Single: £20-£28; both per person per night breakfast included
Open:	Year round
Description:	The Tremont Hotel is set in a tree-lined road just 200 metres from the famous Penzance Promenade and harbour, 10 minutes' walk from the town centre and in easy reach to some of Cornwall's renowned stunning beaches and scenery.
Facilities:	Rooms: ▥ TV General: ⚹✕⌘ Leisure: ▶

POLPERRO

Kirk House ★★★★★Self Catering

Booking: Aspire Lifestyle Holidays,
19 Portland Place East, Leamington Spa CV32 5ES

T:	+44 (0)1503 272320
E:	wts@pierinnholidays.co.uk
W:	kirkhouseholidays.co.uk
Units:	1 • sleeps 10
Prices:	From £700-£2,000 per week
Open:	Year round
Description:	Kirk House is a converted 19thC Methodist chapel, established by Jonathon Couch, "Father of Polperro".
Facilities:	General: ✿

PORTSCATHO

Pollaughan Farm   Self Catering rating applied for

Portscatho, Truro, Cornwall TR2 5EH

T:	+44 (0)1872 580150
E:	pollaughan@yahoo.co.uk
W	pollaughan.co.uk
Units:	4 • sleeps 4
Prices:	From £175-£850 per week
Open:	Year round
Description:	Set on the idyllic Roseland Peninsula with superb sandy beaches nearby and views out over the sea, children and toddlers can feel free and adults can really wind down! A private and tranquil farmstead set in 22 acres of meadows with donkeys, sheep, ducks, buzzards and abundant wildlife.
Facilities:	General: ✿

SITHNEY

Tregoose Farmhouse   ★★★★Self Catering

The Downes, Sithney, Helston, Cornwall TR27 4HW

T:	+44 (0)1736 751749
E:	arcj88@dsl.pipex.com
Units:	1 • sleeps 9
Prices:	From £878-£2,117 per week
Open:	Year round
Description:	A spacious and luxurious former farmhouse in a rural setting. Sleeps nine. Indoor swimming pool and games room. Pets welcome.
Facilities:	General: ✂🛏 Leisure: 🕏

ST GENNYS

Penrowan Farmhouse   ★★★★Self Catering

Booking: Farm & Cottage Holidays, Victoria House, EX39 1AW

T:	+44 (0)1237 479146
E:	enquiries@farmcott.co.uk
W	farmcott.co.uk
Units:	2 • sleeps 6
Prices:	From £215-£500 per week
Open:	Year round
Description:	The pretty, detached stone cottage is set in a quiet position adjacent to the owner's house in a small hamlet not far from the quiet little cove of Crackington Haven, where children can play among the rocks and in the rock pools.
Facilities:	General: 🎲✿ Leisure: ▶

ST MARTIN

Mudgeon Vean Farm ★★★Self Catering
St Martin, Helston, Cornwall, TR12 6DB

T:	+44 (0)1326 231341
E:	mudgeonvean@aol.com
W	cornwall-online.co.uk/mudgeon-vean/welcome.html
Units:	3 • sleeps 8
Prices:	From £115-£425 per week
Open:	Year round
Description:	Three cosy cottages on a small, mixed, 18thC farm. Situated in an Area of Outstanding Natural Beauty close to the Helford River. The farm has panoramic views over an extensive valley area with access to ancient woodland.
Facilities:	General: ✿

ST MERRYN

138 Jasmine Way ★★★Self Catering
Booking: Flat 2, 13 Pinfold Road, London, SW16 2SL

T:	+44 (0) 20 8355 9773
E:	haha.films@virgin.net
W:	cornishselfcateringhols.com
Units:	1 • sleeps 6
Prices:	From £250-£700 per week
Open:	Year round
Description:	In the countryside, near local shops, bars, restaurants, surf, sea and sand. Three bedrooms with bathroom and shower, fully equipped kitchen including washing machine. Safe car parking with front and back garden.
Facilities:	Call for details

ST WENN

Tregolls Farm Cottages ★★★★Self Catering
St Wenn, Bodmin, Cornwall, PL30 5PG

T:	+44 (0) 1208 812154
E:	tregollsfarm@btclick.com
W:	tregollsfarm.co.uk
Units:	4 • sleeps 4
Prices:	From £200-£810 per week • Debit/credit card accepted
Open:	Year round
Description:	Barn conversion holiday homes set in a picturesque valley overlooking fields of cows and sheep.
Facilities:	Room: ☎ General: ✿

STICKER

Glenleigh Farm Fishery ★★★★★Self Catering
Sticker, St Austell, Cornwall, PL26 7JB

T:	+44 (0) 1726 73154
E:	fishglenleigh@aol.com
Units:	1 • sleeps 4
Prices:	From £275-£800 per week
Open:	Year round
Description:	Glenleigh is set in the heart of Cornwall. A perfect rural location, seemingly in the middle of nowhere, but only two minutes off the main A390 through Cornwall.
Facilities:	General: P🐾✿🖵 Leisure: ⌒♪

TINTAGEL

Bosayne Guesthouse ◆◆◆Guest Accommodation
Atlantic Road, Tintagel, Cornwall, PL34 0DE

T:	+44 (0) 1840 770514
E:	kdjewalker@bosayne.wanadoo.co.uk
W:	bosayne.co.uk
Bedrooms:	9 • sleeps 14
Prices:	Double: £25-£30; Single: £23-£30; both per person per night breakfast included • Debit/credit card accepted
Open:	Year round
Description:	A friendly, family-run B&B in the legendary North Cornwall village of Tintagel. Bathing and surfing beaches nearby. Great touring base. Excellent walking and cycling routes for outdoor enthusiasts.
Facilities:	Room: 🖵 General: ✄🛏🅿

TINTAGEL

Brooklets Cottage B&B ★★★★B&B
Bossiney Road, Tintagel, Cornwall, PL34 0AE

T:	+44 (0) 1840 770395
E:	brookletscottage@tiscali.co.uk
W:	brookletscottage.co.uk
Bedrooms:	2 • sleeps 4
Prices:	Double: £25 per person per night breakfast included
Open:	Year round
Description:	Near the heart of Tintagel and ideally situated to explore north Cornwall. Brooklets Cottage offers comfortable accommodation.
Facilities:	Call for details

TRENARREN

Trevissick Manor East Wing ★★★Self Catering
Trevissick Manor, Trenarren, Cornwall PL26 6BQ

T:	+44 (0) 1726 72954
E:	d.treleaven@farmline.com
W:	trevissick.co.uk
Units:	1 • sleeps 5
Prices:	From £250-£500 per week
Open:	Year round
Description:	On farm, manor-house accommodation. Fully equipped, large garden and superb views.
Facilities:	General: ✿

TREYARNON BAY

Treyarnon Bay Youth Hostel ★★★Hostel
Tregonnan, Treyarnon, Padstow, Cornwall, PL28 8JR

T:	+44 (0) 870 770 6076
E:	treyarnon@yha.org.uk
Dormitories:	3 • call for details
Prices:	Dormitory: £7.25-£10.50 per person per night breakfast included • Debit/credit card, cheques/cash accepted
Open:	Year round
Description:	House overlooking sandy cove. A super centre for academic and recreational activities. Perfect for sunsets and surf.
Facilities:	Room: ⓑ✕ⅢⅢ.ⓣⓥ General: ✂P☐✗🚐✕🔌♨ Leisure: ♺

VERYAN

Jago Cottage ★★★★Self Catering
Trewartha, Veryan, Truro, Cornwall, TR2 5QJ

T:	+44 (0) 1872 501491
E:	jago@roseland.me.uk
W:	roseland.me.uk
Units:	1 • sleeps 2
Prices:	From £280-£600 per week
Open:	Year round
Description:	Special self-contained accommodation ideally situated in the Roseland Peninsula, miles of sandy beaches and stunning coastal walks to explore.
Facilities:	Call for details

AMBLESIDE

Claremont House ◆◆◆◆Guest Accommodation

Compston Road, Ambleside, Cumbria, LA22 9DJ

T:	+44 (0) 1539 433448
E:	enquiries@claremontambleside.co.uk
W:	claremontambleside.co.uk
Bedrooms:	6 • sleeps 16
Prices:	Double: £25-£33 per person per night breakfast included Debit/credit card accepted
Open:	Year round
Description:	A warm welcome awaits you at Claremont House, where you will enjoy good food and hospitality. The house is a typical Victorian building of Lakeland stone, modernised carefully to preserve its original character.
Facilities:	Room: 🛏, General: ✂

AMBLESIDE

Hatter's Cottage ★★★Self Catering

Booking: Hawkshead Hill Farm, Hawkshead Hill, Cumbria, LA22 0PW

T:	+44 (0) 1539 436203
E:	mail22@hatterscottage.co.uk
W:	hatterscottage.co.uk
Units:	1 • sleeps 5
Prices:	From £210-£450 per week
Open:	Year round
Description:	Hatter's Cottage is an 18thC stone cottage in a secluded location 150m from public roads on a small farm near a hilltop between Coniston and Windermere lakes.
Facilities:	General: P✂❄▣

AMBLESIDE

Melrose Guesthouse ★★★★Guest Accommodation

Church Street, Ambleside, Cumbria, LA22 0BT

T:	+44 (0) 1539 432500
E:	info@melrose-guesthouse.co.uk
W:	melrose-guesthouse.co.uk
Bedrooms:	8 • sleeps 15
Prices:	Double and single rooms: £29-£44 per person per night breakfast included • Euros accepted
Open:	Year round
Description:	Elegant stone terraced Victorian House set out over four floors. Peacefully situated near the centre of Ambleside with all shops and restaurants just two minutes' stroll away.
Facilities:	Room: 🛏, General: ✂▣❄

CUMBRIA

AMBLESIDE

Nab Cottage ◆◆◆ Guest Accommodation
Rydal, Ambleside, Cumbria, LA22 9SD

T:	+44 (0) 1539 435311
E:	tim@nabcottage.com
W:	rydalwater.com
Bedrooms:	6 • sleeps 14
Prices:	Double: £25-£28 per person per night breakfast included Debit/credit card, euros accepted
Open:	Year round
Description:	A 16thC farmhouse once owned by Thomas de Quincey. Four rooms with lake view, log fires, homemade bread, organic produce where possible.
Facilities:	Rooms: 🛏️📺 General: ⅍P📶🍷✕☼🐾

AMBLESIDE

Rothay Garth ★★★★ Guest Accommodation
Rothay Road, Ambleside, Cumbria, LA22 0EE

T:	+44 (0) 1539 432217
E:	book@rothay-garth.co.uk
W:	rothay-garth.co.uk
Bedrooms:	14 • sleeps 28
Prices:	Double: £33.50-£60 per person per night breakfast included Debit/credit card accepted
Open:	Year round
Description:	Rothay Garth has a superb position combining glorious mountain views with easy access to Windermere Lake and Ambleside.
Facilities:	Rooms: 🛏️ General: P📶🍷☼🐾 Leisure: ▶

AMBLESIDE

Rothay Manor ★★★ Hotel
SILVER AWARD
Rothay Bridge, Ambleside, Cumbria, LA22 0EH

T:	+44 (0) 1539 433605
E:	hotel@rothaymanor.co.uk
W:	rothaymanor.co.uk
Bedrooms:	12 • sleeps 25
Prices:	Double: £73-£110; Single: £85-£90; both per person per night breakfast included • Debit/credit card accepted
Open:	Year round
Description:	An elegant Regency country house hotel set in its own landscaped gardens 0.25 miles from Lake Windermere and a short walk from the centre of Ambleside, making Rothay Manor an ideal base for walking or sightseeing.
Facilities:	Rooms: 🛏️📺 General: P🍷✕☼🐾 Leisure: ⊔▶

AMBLESIDE

Thorneyfield Guesthouse ★★★Guesthouse
Compston Road, Ambleside, Cumbria, LA22 9DJ

T:	+44 (0) 1539 432464
E:	info@thorneyfield.co.uk
W:	thorneyfield.co.uk
Bedrooms:	5 • sleeps 13
Prices:	Double: £28-£32 per person per night breakfast included Debit/credit card accepted
Open:	Year round
Description:	Alison and Alan Davis are proud to welcome you to Thorneyfield, which is a charming, Victorian period property set in the heart of Ambleside and the beautiful Lake District.
Facilities:	Rooms: ▥ General: ⚥P✗

ASPATRIA

Big White House ★★★Self Catering
Booking: Skiddaw View Holiday Home Park Ltd, Bothel, CA7 2JG

T:	+44 (0) 1697 320919
E:	info@bigwhitehouse.co.uk
W:	bigwhitehouse.co.uk/ctb
Bedrooms:	9 • sleeps 18
Prices:	From £953-£2,038 per week • Debit/credit card accepted
Open:	Year round
Description:	Accommodating up to 18 people in 9 bedrooms, an excellent venue for parties and social gatherings. Sitting in an acre of private grounds there is secure storage for bikes and canoes as well as plenty of parking.
Facilities:	Rooms: ☏ General: P▥✿☕⊚ Leisure: ∪♣▶

BLACKFORD

Metal Bridge House ★★★★B&B
Metal Bridge, Blackford, Carlisle, Cumbria, CA6 4HG

T:	+44 (0) 1228 674695
E:	info@metal-bridge-house.co.uk
W:	metal-bridge-house.co.uk
Bedrooms:	3 • sleeps 5
Prices:	Double: £45-£55; Single: £35-£45; both per person per night breakfast included
Open:	Year round
Description:	Quiet yet close to M6 and A74. Handy for a one night stopover or a week's stay. Lounge or beautiful garden to sit and relax in. Walk along the banks of the River Esk.
Facilities:	Room: ▥ General: ◑⚥P✿᠑ Leisure: ∪▶

BLINDCRAKE

Ghyll Yeat ★★★★Self Catering

Booking: 1 Park Villas, Keswick, CA12 5LQ

T:	+44 (0) 1768 780321
E:	peter_anneghyllyeat@lineone.net
W:	ghyllyeat.co.uk
Units:	1 • sleeps 4
Prices:	From £215-£370 per week
Open:	Year round
Description:	Tranquil cottage of character close to Cockermouth/ Bassenthwaite in the picturesque village of Blindcrake. Situated within the Lake District National Park offering good access to the Northern Fells and Solway Coast.
Facilities:	General: P

BOWNESS-ON-WINDERMERE

Lindeth Howe Country House Hotel ★★★Hotel

Lindeth Drive, Longtail Hill, Windermere, Cumbria, LA23 3JF SILVER AWARD

T:	+44 (0) 1539 445759
E:	hotel@lindeth-howe.co.uk
W:	lindeth-howe.co.uk
Bedrooms:	26 • sleeps 56
Prices:	Double: £200-£210 per room per night breakfast included Debit/credit card, euros accepted
Open:	Year round
Description:	Lindeth Howe Country House is a tranquil retreat situated one mile south of Bowness-on-Windermere. Set in six acres of stunning gardens, located on a hillside with spectacular views of Lake Windermere and the Fells beyond.
Facilities:	Rooms: TV General: Leisure:

BRIDEKIRK

Anns Hill ★★★★★Self Catering

Anns Hill, Bridekirk, Cockermouth, CA13 0NY

T:	07710 388180
E:	vanessa@annshill.co.uk
W:	annshill.co.uk
Units:	1 • sleeps 2
Prices:	From £560-£625 per week • Debit/credit card accepted
Open:	Year round
Description:	Plasma TV, Bose music system, wireless broadband, fabulously equipped kitchen, stone spiral staircase, spacious sitting room with log burner, super king-sized 6ft bed, full oil-fired central heating.
Facilities:	Rooms: TV General: P Leisure:

CARK IN CARTMEL

Grange End Cottage ★★★★ Self Catering

Booking: 45 The Row, Silverdale, LA5 0UG

T:	+44 (0) 1524 702955
E:	stc@2fs.com
W:	holidaycottagescumbria.com
Units:	2 • sleeps 12
Prices:	From £112-£950 per week • Debit/credit card, euros accepted
Open:	Year round
Description:	A charming and luxurious 18thC cottage, furnished with antiques and four-poster bed. Price includes gas, electricity, logs, bed linen and towels. Only one mile from historic Cartmel village and 10 minutes from Lake Windermere.
Facilities:	Rooms: ☎ General: P🅿❊▣ Leisure: ⋃►

COCKERMOUTH

Cockermouth YHA ★★ Hostel

Double Mills, Fern Bank Road, Cockermouth, Cumbria, CA13 0DS

T:	+44 (0) 1900 822561
E:	cockermouth@yha.org.uk
Dormitories:	3 • sleeps 26
Prices:	Dormitory pricing: £7-£11 • Debit/credit card accepted
Open:	Year round
Description:	17thC watermill in secluded riverside location. Parents should be aware young children should be watched while in grounds. YHA membership is required. Reception open 17.00-22.30.
Facilities:	General: ✕P🅿

CONISTON

Orchard Cottage ♦♦♦♦ Guest Accommodation

18 Yewdale Road, Coniston, Cumbria, LA21 8DU

T:	+44 (0) 1539 441319
E:	enquiries@conistonholidays.co.uk
W:	conistonholidays.co.uk
Bedrooms:	3 • sleeps 6
Prices:	Double: £28 per person per night breakfast included Debit/credit card accepted
Open:	Year round
Description:	Orchard Cottage is centrally situated in Coniston village. Excellent accommodation with three attractive en suite rooms all on ground level. Tea-/coffee-making facilities. Guest lounge with TV, separate dining room.
Facilities:	Room: ▥ General: ✕P🅿❊

DENT

The George & Dragon Hotel ★★★Inn
Main Street, Dent, Sedbergh, Cumbria, LA10 5QL

T:	+44 (0) 1539 625256
E:	TheGeorgeandDragon@tiscali.co.uk
W:	thegeorgeanddragondent.co.uk
Bedrooms:	9 • sleeps 22
Prices:	Double: £29.50-£37.50 per person per night breakfast included
	Debit/credit card accepted
Open:	Year round
Description:	The George & Dragon is situated in the centre of Dent village overlooking the famous Adam Sedgewick Memorial Fountain. Traditionally furnished with two relaxing public rooms and restaurant serving home-cooked food.
Facilities:	Room: 🛏️📺
	General: ●🍴🛜✕🎵
	Leisure: ∪🚲▶

DRUMBURGH

The Grange ★★★★Self Catering
Grange Cottages, Drumburgh, Carlisle, CA7 5DW

T:	+44 (0) 1228 576551
E:	messrs.hodgson@tesco.net
W:	thegrangecottage.co.uk
Units:	2 • sleeps 6
Prices:	From £160-£290 per week • Euros accepted
Open:	Year round
Description:	Drumburgh is a hamlet beside the Solway Firth, in an area of outstanding natural beauty. Hadrian's Wall National Trail is close by, ending in Bowness-on-Solway. The RSPB reserve and nature reserves are also nearby.
Facilities:	General: P✣📷
	Leisure: ∪▶

EDENHALL

Eden House Loft ★★★★Self Catering
10 Renwick Lane, Cardrona, EH45 9LU

T:	+44 (0) 1896 831547
E:	dom@elfino.com
Units:	1 • sleeps 2
Prices:	From £200-£300 per week
Open:	Year round
Description:	Detached loft-style studio in Eden Valley with pub. Well placed to explore Ullswater, Eden Valley and North Pennines.
Facilities:	General: P✣📷

ESKDALE

Randle How ★★★★ Self Catering

Booking: Long Yocking How, Eskdale, Cumbria, CA19 1UA

T:	+44 (0) 1946 723126
E:	js.wedley@btopenworld.com
Units:	1 • sleeps 4
Prices:	From £225-£425 per week
Open:	Year round
Description:	An 18thC cottage with modern facilities. A large attractive garden. Situated in a quiet lane but only five minutes from shop. Walks from the door. Eskdale & Ravenglass station three minutes' walk.
Facilities:	General: P✾回

HUTTON ROOF

Dukes Meadow ★★★ Self Catering

Booking: 5 Upwey Avenue, Solihull, B91 1LR

T:	+44 (0) 121 705 4381
E:	janeandben@hotmail.co.uk
W:	dukesmeadow.co.uk
Units:	1 • sleeps 6
Prices:	From £150-£450 per week
Open:	Year round
Description:	Three-bedroom holiday lodge, recently refurbished to a high standard in peaceful location. Good base for the north Lakes and Eden Valley and within easy reach of the excellent facilities in Penrith. Short breaks available.
Facilities:	Room: ☎ General: **P**

KENDAL

The County Hotel ★★ Townhouse Hotel

Station Road, Kendal, Cumbria, LA9 6BT

T:	+44 (0) 1539 722461
Bedrooms:	37 • sleeps 77
Prices:	Double: £64-£86 per room per night breakfast included; Single: £32-£43 per person per night breakfast included Debit/credit card, cheques/cash accepted
Open:	Year round except Christmas and New Year
Description:	The County Hotel dates to the pre-1780s.
Facilities:	Room: ☎🛏️📺♿ General: ●✂🕎🚗×🅿

KESWICK

Allerdale House ★★★★Guesthouse

1 Eskin Street, Keswick, Cumbria, CA12 4DH

T:	+44 (0) 1768 773891
E:	allerdalehouse@btinternet.com
W:	allerdale-house.co.uk
Bedrooms:	6 • sleeps 11
Prices:	Double: £28-£50; Single: £30-£50; both per person per night breakfast included • Debit/credit card, euros accepted
Open:	Year round except New Year
Description:	Allerdale House is close to the centre of the picturesque market town of Keswick with its pubs, restaurants and shops. Derwentwater is only five minutes' walk away and it is within walking distance of the northern Fells.
Facilities:	Room: 🛏️, 📺 General: ✂P☕🍽✕🐾

KESWICK

Appletrees ★★★★Guesthouse

The Heads, Keswick, Cumbria, CA12 5ER

T:	+44 (0) 1768 780400
E:	john@armstrong2001.fsnet.co.uk
W:	appletreeskeswick.com
Bedrooms:	7 • sleeps 13
Prices:	Double: £27-£35; Single: £30-£35; both per person per night breakfast included • Debit/credit card accepted
Open:	Year round
Description:	Strictly non-smoking. Spacious Victorian house recently refurbished with spectacular views. Friendly hosts. Full English breakfast. Ideal location close to town centre, lake, park and theatre.
Facilities:	Room: 🛏️, General: ✂☒P

KESWICK

Bramblewood Cottage Guesthouse ★★★ B&B

2 Greta Street, Keswick, Cumbria, CA12 4HS

T:	+44 (0) 1768 775918
E:	dorothy@dorothybell.wanadoo.co.uk
W:	bramblewoodkeswick.com
Bedrooms:	6 • sleeps 12
Prices:	Double: £27-£35 per person per night breakfast included
Open:	Year round
Description:	Beautiful 200-year-old cottage overlooking Fitz Park with stunning views of the River Greta, Skiddaw and Latrigg. Children very welcome, aged seven years plus. Arrival times between 15.00-18.00 and prior by arrangement.
Facilities:	General: ✂P☒

KESWICK

Sandon Guesthouse   ♦♦♦♦ Guest Accommodation

Southey Street, Keswick, Cumbria, CA12 4EG

T:	+44 (0) 1768 773648
E:	enquiries@sandonguesthouse.com
W:	sandonguesthouse.com

Bedrooms:	6 • sleeps 10
Prices:	Double and single rooms: £25-£30 per person per night breakfast included
Open:	Year round
Description:	A lovingly restored Victorian stone townhouse situated in a lovely garden. We aim to provide comfortable, friendly accommodation.
Facilities:	Room: 🛏 General: ✂☙❀

KESWICK

Sunnyside Guesthouse   ★★★★ Guesthouse

25 Southey Street, Keswick, Cumbria, CA12 4EF

T:	+44 (0) 1768 772446
E:	enquiries@sunnysideguesthouse.com
W:	sunnysideguesthouse.com

Bedrooms:	7 • sleeps 16
Prices:	Double: £28-£31.50; Single £30-£31.50; both per person per night breakfast included • Debit/credit card accepted
Open:	Year round
Description:	Large Victorian house with private car park in a quiet position approximately three minutes from the town centre. All rooms are very well furnished with either en suite or private facilities.
Facilities:	Room: 🛏 General: ✂P🅿

MOORHOUSE

Low Moor House   ★★★★ Self Catering

Manor Croft, Moorhouse, CA5 6EL

T:	+44 (0) 1228 575153
E:	info@lowmoorhouse.co.uk
W:	lowmoorhouse.co.uk

Units:	1 • sleeps 9
Prices:	From £490-£1,560 per week
Open:	Year round
Description:	Low Moor House has been a splendid family home for the past 16 years. It is on the little-known Solway Plain to the west of Carlisle.
Facilities:	General: P☙❀🖵 Leisure: ►

NATEBY

The Black Bull ★★★★Inn

Nateby, Kirkby Stephen, Cumbria, CA17 4JP

T:	+44 (0) 1768 371588
E:	blackbullinn@hotmail.com
Bedrooms:	5 • sleeps 10
Prices:	Double: £28-£32 per person per night breakfast included Debit/credit card accepted
Open:	Year round
Description:	Recently refurbished country inn at the entrance to the Dales. Many walks accessible from the inn. Centrally located for visiting both Lakes and Dales National Parks. Fine ales and excellent home-made food served in the bar and restaurant.
Facilities:	Room: 🏠📺 General: P🍺🚌✕ Leisure: ⚑

NEW HUTTON

1 Ashes Barn ★★★★Guest Accommodation

New Hutton, Kendal, Cumbria, LA8 0AS

T:	+44 (0) 1539 729215
Bedrooms:	3 • sleeps 6
Prices:	Double: £26-£30 per person per night room only Debit/credit card, euros accepted
Open:	Year round
Description:	Ashes Barn is a recent barn conversion, which offers all the comforts of modern life combined with the character of a traditional Lake District building. Set in the heart of the countryside, the house enjoys delightful rural views.
Facilities:	Room: ✕🍴🛁🏠📺🕭 General: ✂P🅿✕☼🅜

NEWLANDS

Bawd Hall ★★★★★Self Catering

Booking: High Mosser Gate, Mosser, CA13 0SR

T:	+44 (0) 1900 828189
E:	alison@bawdhall.co.uk
W:	bawdhall.co.uk
Units:	5 • sleeps 10
Prices:	From £600-£1,650 per week
Open:	Year round
Description:	Luxury country house with superb views. Excellent walking area 15 minutes from Keswick. Five bedrooms and four bathrooms, large lounge, open fire, garden room, large kitchen/dining room, utility, central heating, double-glazing and cycle storage.
Facilities:	Room: 🏠 General: P🅿☼🅙

NEWLANDS

Ellas Crag ◆◆◆◆Guest Accommodation

Newlands Valley, Keswick, Cumbria, CA12 5TS

T:	+44 (0) 1768 778217
E:	ellascrag@talk21.com
W:	ellascrag.co.uk
Bedrooms:	4 • sleeps 8
Prices:	Double: £31-£35 per person per night breakfast included
Open:	Year round
Description:	Ellas Crag is built of Lakeland stone, set on the lower slopes of Causey Pike. The house enjoys commanding views over Newlands Valley, towards Catbells opposite and Siddaw to the east. Less than 10 minutes from Keswick centre.
Facilities:	Room: 🛏️ General: ✳P✿🐾

PORTINSCALE

Woodside ★★★★Self Catering

Low Portinscale, Portinscale, Keswick, CA12 5RP

T:	+44 (0) 1768 772212
E:	paulandrew40@hotmail.com
Units:	1 • sleeps 8
Prices:	From £180-£510 per week
Open:	Year round
Description:	Four-bedroom, end-of-terrace, recently renovated, Lakeland cottage sleeps eight. Stunning views of Skiddaw, parking for two cars, garden with large deck. Ideal base for exploring the northern Fells.
Facilities:	General: P✿🖥️

RAVENSTONEDALE

Westview ★★★★B&B

Ravenstonedale, Kirkby Stephen, Cumbria, CA17 4NG

T:	+44 (0) 1539 623415
Bedrooms:	3 • sleeps 6
Prices:	Double: £22.27 per person per night breakfast included
Open:	Year round
Description:	Westview has been fully refurbished to a high standard. There are beautiful views to Wild Boar and Green from the conservatory. The dining room overlooks the village green. Ample parking to the rear.
Facilities:	Room: 🛏️ General: ✳P✿ Leisure: ▶

ROSTHWAITE

Hazel Bank ◆◆◆◆◆ Guest Accommodation

Rosthwaite, Borrowdale, Keswick, Cumbria, CA12 5XB   GOLD AWARD

T:	+44 (0) 1768 777248
E:	enquiries@hazelbankhotel.co.uk
W:	hazelbankhotel.co.uk
Bedrooms:	1 • sleeps 2
Prices:	Double: £33.50-£62.50 per person per night breakfast included • Debit/credit card accepted
Open:	Year round
Description:	Award-winning Hazel Bank, an early Victorian country house, stands secluded and peacefully amid beautiful four-acre gardens with breathtaking views of Great Gable and other central Lakeland fells. Recently refurbished.
Facilities:	Room: 🖵 General: ⚡P🕮🍷⚒✕❄🏵 Leisure: U🚵🏇

SEATHWAITE

Hall Dunnerdale Farm Holiday Cottages   Self Catering

Booking: Dove Bank House, Kirkby-in-Furness, LA17 7XD

T:	+44 (0) 1229 889281
E:	anne@hall-dunnerdale.co.uk
Units:	4 • sleeps 16
Prices:	From £255-£560 per week
Open:	Year round except Christmas and New Year
Description:	Set in the beautiful, unspoilt Duddon Valley, at the heart of the English Lake District, Hall Dunnerdale offers traditional Lake District cottages that are second to none.
Facilities:	Call for details

SEATOLLER

Honister Hause YHA ★★★ Hostel

Seatoller, Keswick, Cumbria, CA12 5XN

T:	+44 (0) 1768 777267
E:	honister@yha.org.uk
W:	yha.org.uk/hostel/hostelpages/265.html
Dormitories:	Call for details
Prices:	Dormitory pricing: £13-£15 • Debit/credit card accepted
Open:	Year round except New Year
Description:	Great for dedicated walkers who are at home on the hills. Situated next to the working Honister Slate Mine this former quarry workers' building is in a spectacular setting at the summit of Honister Pass, a high-level route connecting the valleys of Borrowdale and Buttermere.
Facilities:	Room: 🛏✕🖵📺 General: ⚡P🕮🍷⚒✕🏵

THORNTHWAITE

Comb Beck
★★★ Self Catering

Booking: Moss Garth, Braithwaite, CA12 5SX

T:	+44 (0) 1768 778097
E:	jacquidmoss@aol.com
W:	lakedistrict-cottage.com
Units:	1 • sleeps 4
Prices:	From £200-£450 per week
Open:	Year round
Description:	Cosy, old stone cottage, fully heated throughout with open fire in the lounge. Garden with beck and bridge across. Views. Direct access to Fells and Whinlatter Visitor Centre. Available from 3pm exit by 10am. Secure bike shed.
Facilities:	Room: 🛏️ General: P♨☼

TORVER

Wilson Arms
★★★ Inn

Torver, Coniston, Cumbria, LA21 8BB

T:	+44 (0) 1539 441237
Bedrooms:	8 • sleeps 19
Prices:	Double: £27-£35; Single: £30-£35; both per person per night breakfast included • Debit/credit card accepted
Open:	Year round
Description:	Family-run country inn. Central heating, log fires. Good location for touring the Lakes. Good food. Cosy bar.
Facilities:	Room: 🛏️📺 General: P♨✗☼ Leisure: ∪🚲

TROUTBECK

Gill Head Farm
★★★★ Farmhouse

Troutbeck, Penrith, Cumbria, CA11 0ST

T:	+44 (0) 1768 779652
E:	enquiries@gillheadfarm.co.uk
W:	gillheadfarm.co.uk
Bedrooms:	5 • sleeps 10
Prices:	Double: £27 per person per night breakfast included
Open:	Year round except Christmas and New Year
Description:	Gill Head is a working farm set against the spectacular backdrop of Blencathra and the northern Fells.
Facilities:	Room: 🛏️ General: 🏕️🖪 Leisure: 🚲♟

WIGTON

Middleton's/Fountain Cottage ★★★ Self Catering

Booking: The Old Rectory, Litlington, BN26 5RB

T:	+44 (0) 1323 870032
E:	candpayers@mistral.co.uk
W:	dentcottages.co.uk
Units:	2 • sleeps 8
Prices:	From £190-£310 per week
Open:	Year round
Description:	Both cottages have been carefully modernised and tastefully furnished to a high standard.
Facilities:	General: P✿⊚

WINDERMERE

Oakfold House ★★★★B&B

Beresford Road, Windermere, Bowness, Cumbria, LA23 2JG

T:	+44 (0) 1539 443239
E:	oakfoldhouse@fsmail.net
W:	oakfoldhouse.co.uk
Bedrooms:	6 • sleeps 12
Prices:	Double: £25-£40; Single: £30-£40; both per person per night breakfast included • Debit/credit card, euros accepted
Open:	Year round
Description:	Beautiful Victorian guesthouse with many original features situated within a few minutes walk of Lake Windermere and amenities of Bowness. Recently restored and refurbished. Lovely garden and private car park. Non-smoking.
Facilities:	Room: ▥, General: ✘P✗✿

ALDERWASLEY

Wiggonlea Stable ★★★★Self Catering

Wiggonlea Farm, Alderwasley, Belper, Derbyshire, DE56 2RE

T:	+44 (0) 1773 852344
E:	ruth@wiggonlea.fsnet.co.uk
W:	wiggonlea.fsnet.co.uk
Units:	1 • sleeps 4
Prices:	From £190-£350 per week
Open:	Year round
Description:	Tastefully converted stable on working farm, retaining lots of character with log burner and open beams. Set in glorious countryside adjacent to Shining Cliff Woods with its many footpaths. Easy access to all Derbyshire attractions.
Facilities:	General: P✿ Leisure: ☍

BUXTON

Kingscroft Guesthouse ♦♦♦♦ Guest Accommodation

Green Lane, Buxton, Derbyshire, SK17 9DP

T:	+44 (0) 1298 22757
W:	kings-croft@btopenworld.com
Bedrooms:	8 • sleeps 15
Prices:	Double: £30-£35; Single: £30-£40; both per person per night breakfast included
Open:	Year round
Description:	We welcome you to stay in our late Victorian luxury guesthouse, in a central, yet quiet, position in Buxton. Here you will find everything you need for a relaxing break in comfortable surroundings with period decor and furnishings.
Facilities:	Room: 📺 General: P🛏🍽✕❄🎵

BUXTON

Linden Lodge ★★★★B&B

31 Temple Road, Buxton, Derbyshire, SK17 9BA

T:	+44 (0) 1298 27591
W:	LindenTreeLodge.co.uk
Bedrooms:	2 • sleeps 4
Prices:	Double: £24-£26 per person per night breakfast included
Open:	Year round
Description:	Friendly and homely quality accommodation in a quiet, residential area for guests to relax and enjoy the beauty of Buxton and the surrounding countryside. A warm welcome awaits you. Guest lounge with TV/video & CD player.
Facilities:	Room: 🛏 General: ✄P❄🎵

BUXTON

Stoneridge ♦♦♦♦ Guest Accommodation

9 Park Road, Buxton, Derbyshire, SK17 6SG — SILVER AWARD

T:	+44 (0) 1298 26120
E:	duncan@stoneridge.co.uk
W:	stoneridge.co.uk
Bedrooms:	4 • sleeps 8
Prices:	Double: £25 per person per night breakfast included
Open:	Year round
Description:	High quality Silver Award, licensed accommodation set in a peaceful location just three minutes' walk from the Opera House. Pristine and homely. All rooms en suite with private off-road car parking. Evening meals available.
Facilities:	Room: 🛏 General: ✄P🍽❄🎵

CHAPEL-EN-LE-FRITH

High Croft ◆◆◆◆◆Guest Accommodation

Manchester Road, Chapel-en-le-Frith, High Peak, Derbyshire, SK23 9UH

T:	+44 (0) 1298 814843
E:	elaine@highcroft-guesthouse.co.uk
W:	highcroft-guesthouse.co.uk
Bedrooms:	5 • sleeps 12
Prices:	Double: £27.50-£38 per person per night breakfast included
Open:	Year round
Description:	Just a 10 minute drive from Buxton, High Croft is a luxurious Edwardian Country House set in 1.5 acres of peaceful, mature gardens adjoining Chapel-en-le-Frith golf course and Combs Reservoir. All rooms have fabulous views over the Peak Park and superb walks directly from the front door.
Facilities:	General: ✿ Leisure: ▶

COMBS

Pyegreave Cottage ★★★★★Self Catering

Combs SK23 9UX

T:	+44 (0) 1298 813444
E:	n.pollard@allenpollard.co.uk
Units:	1 • sleeps 2
Prices:	From £260-395 per week • Debit/credit card, euros accepted
Open:	Year round
Description:	Peak District cottage with spectacular views and many interesting features. Centrally heated and finished to a high standard.
Facilities:	Room: ▥ General: P✄✿▣

CRESSBROOK

1 The Old Hay Barn ★★★★★Guest Accommodation

The Barns, Cressbrook, Buxton, Derbyshire, SK17 8SY

T:	+44 (0) 1298 873503
E:	dcmacb@aol.com
Bedrooms:	1 • sleeps 2
Prices:	Double: £25 per person per night breakfast included
Open:	Year round
Description:	Luxury accommodation in beautiful setting overlooking river and lake. Exclusive suite comprising bedroom, bathroom, sitting room furnished to high standard. Excellent local pub/restaurants. Four miles from Bakewell, Chatsworth.
Facilities:	General: ✔P▥✿

ELTON

Homestead Farm ◆◆◆◆Guest Accommodation

Main Street, Elton, Matlock, Derbyshire, DE4 2BW

T:	+44 (0) 1629 650359
W:	homesteadfarm.co.uk
Bedrooms:	1 • sleeps 2
Prices:	Double: £18-£20 per person per night breakfast included
Open:	Year round
Description:	Accommodation for B&B is within the farmhouse dating to the early 1800s. It has one double en suite bedroom (with private toilet), complete with colour TV, tea-/coffee-making facilities and two easy chairs.
Facilities:	Room: ♿📺 General: P✕☼🅿

FENNY BENTLEY

Millfields ★★★B&B

Fenny Bentley, Ashbourne, Derbyshire, DE6 1LA

T:	+44 (0) 1335 350454
W:	millfieldsbandb.co.uk
Bedrooms:	3 • sleeps 6
Prices:	Double: £25 per person per night breakfast included
Open:	Year round
Description:	Situated in Fenny Bentley Village on a small holding overlooking Peak Park Trail and Dovedale. Convenient for Alton Towers. Excellent breakfast serving free-range eggs. Inn serving meals 150 yards away.
Facilities:	Room: 🛏 General: ✕P☼🅿 Leisure: ♾

HARTINGTON

Cotesfield Farm ★★Farmhouse

Parsley Hay, Buxton, Derbyshire, SK17 0BD

T:	+44 (0) 1298 83256
Bedrooms:	3 • sleeps 6
Prices:	Double: £20-£25 per person per night breakfast included Euros accepted
Open:	Year round
Description:	On the High Peak trail overlooking Upper Long Dale and offering peace and quiet on a working farm.
Facilities:	Room: ♿🛏 General: 🏠🅿☼🅿

HARTINGTON

The Charles Cotton Hotel ★★ Hotel

Market Place, Hartington, Buxton, Derbyshire, SK17 0AL

T:	+44 (0) 1298 84229
E:	info@charlescotton.co.uk
W:	charlescotton.co.uk
Bedrooms:	17 • sleeps 38
Prices:	Double: £37.50; Single: £45; both per person per night breakfast included • Debit/credit card accepted
Open:	Year round
Description:	Family-run hotel serving good food and real ales, ideal base for walking, cycling and Alton Towers. Children and pets welcome. Hotel has own gift shop and tea rooms.
Facilities:	Room: 📺 General: P🍴🚐✕❄

HOPE

Underleigh House ♦♦♦♦♦ Guest Accommodation

off Edale Road, Hope, Hope Valley, Derbyshire, S33 6RF　　GOLD AWARD

T:	+44 (0) 1433 621372
E:	info@underleighhouse.co.uk
W:	underleighhouse.co.uk
Bedrooms:	6 • sleeps 12
Prices:	Double: £33-£36 per person per night breakfast included Debit/credit card accepted
Open:	Year round
Description:	Secluded cottage and barn conversion near the village with magnificent countryside views. Ideal for walking and exploring the Peak District. Delicious breakfasts featuring local and homemade specialities. Welcoming and relaxing.
Facilities:	General: ✗P🍴❄📺 Leisure: 🚴

MATLOCK

Rosegarth ♦♦♦♦ Guest Accommodation

57 Dimple Road, Matlock, Derbyshire, DE4 3JX

T:	+44 (0) 1629 56294
E:	john@crich.ndo.co.uk
W:	rosegarthmatlock.co.uk
Bedrooms:	2 • sleeps 2
Prices:	Double: £50-£55 room per night breakfast included
Open:	Year round
Description:	Rosegarth is a charming cottage in the heart of the Derbyshire Dales, close to the Peak District. Situated within walking distance of Matlock town centre, bus and train stations and all amenities.
Facilities:	General: ✗P❄

NEW MILLS

Shaw Farm Cottage ★★Self Catering

Shaw Marsh SK22 4QE

T:	+44 (0) 161 427 1841
E:	nicky.burgess@talk21.com
W:	shawfarmholidays.co.uk
Units:	1 • sleeps – Call for details
Prices:	From £270-520 per week
Open:	Year round
Description:	A three-bedroomed farmhouse with character, set in open countryside. Price reduced if family bedroom not required. Garden with patio. Children's play area. Please apply for brochure or see web advert.
Facilities:	General: P❖ Leisure: �

RIPLEY

Bowling Green B&B ♦♦♦Guest Accommodation

Blacksmiths Croft, Ripley, Derbyshire, DE5 8JL

T:	+44 (0) 1773 742921
Bedrooms:	1 • sleeps 2
Prices:	Double: £25 per person per night breakfast included Euros accepted
Open:	Year round
Description:	Three-storey, semi-detached new townhouse, within walking distance of Ripley town centre and five minute drive to Denby Pottery Visitor Centre. Marehay Bowling Club green is adjacent.
Facilities:	Room: TV General: ⚡PX❖✉

STANTON-IN-THE-PEAK

Rock House ★★★Self Catering

Booking: PACCS Ltd, Unit 8a, Meverill Road, Buxton, SK17 8PY

T:	+44 (0) 1298 872418
E:	paul@rockhouse-peakdistrict.co.uk
W:	rockhouse-peakdistrict.co.uk
Units:	1 • sleeps 5
Prices:	From £245-450 per week • Debit/credit card, euros accepted
Open:	Year round
Description:	Comfortable, well-equipped gritstone cottage in Peak Park village, but close to many popular attractions and walks. Solid fuel central heating, linen provided, safe, dry bike storage, conservatory, small fish pond and off-road parking.
Facilities:	Room: ▥ General: P▣▤

STURSTON

The Old Laundry ★★★★★ Self Catering

Booking: Sturston Hall, Mill Lane, Ashbourne, DE6 1LN

T:	+44 (0) 1335 346711
E:	p.cust@virgin.net
W:	sturston.com
Units:	1 • sleeps – Call for details
Prices:	From £300-£500 per week
Open:	Year round
Description:	The Old Laundry, a converted Grade II Listed barn, is a wing of owners' 17thC house, in secluded valley, on quiet lane close to Ashbourne. Many original features; beamed ceilings, wood and brick floors and stone mullioned windows.
Facilities:	Room: ☎ General: P✿

TIDESWELL

Markeygate Cottages ★★★★ Self Catering

Markeygate Cottages, Bank Square, Buxton, SK17 8NT

T:	+44 (0) 1298 871260
E:	markeygatehouse@hotmail.com
W:	markeygatecottages.co.uk
Units:	2 • sleeps 6
Prices:	From £175-£355 per week
Open:	Year round
Description:	Two charming character cottages, Grade II Listed, tastefully furnished, modern comprehensively equipped. Features gritstone fireplace, beams, open fire and central heating.
Facilities:	Room: ▥ General: ✿⚐

TISSINGTON

Bassett Wood Farm ♦♦♦♦ Guest Accommodation

Tissington, Ashbourne, Derbyshire, DE6 1RD

T:	+44 (0) 1335 350254
E:	janet@bassettwood.freeserve.co.uk
Bedrooms:	3 • sleeps 3
Prices:	Double: £30 per person per night breakfast included Debit/credit card accepted
Open:	Year round
Description:	Bassett Wood Farm B&B is four diamond standard with en suite rooms and four-poster beds.
Facilities:	Room: ▤ General: ⊬✿ Leisure: ♃

WYASTON

White Cottage ♦♦♦♦ Guest Accommodation

White Cottage, Derbyshire, Ashbourne, Derbyshire, DE6 2DR

T:	+44 (0) 1335 345503
E:	jackie@previll.fsnet.co.uk
W:	whitecottage-bandb.co.uk
Bedrooms:	1 • sleeps 2
Prices:	Double: £24-£25 per person per night breakfast included
Open:	Year round
Description:	Large, character cottage in quiet rural village. Lovely views over countryside. Beautifully decorated ground floor room overlooking large, secluded garden for guests' relaxation.
Facilities:	Room: 🛏️ General: ⚷P✿

YOULGRAVE

The Farmyard Inn ♦♦♦ Guest Accommodation

Main Street, Youlgrave, Bakewell, Derbyshire, DE45 1UW

T:	+44 (0) 1629 636221
Bedrooms:	3 • sleeps 6
Prices:	Double: £45 per room per night breakfast included Debit/credit card accepted
Open:	Year round
Description:	Situated in Peak District, close to Haddon Hall and Chatsworth. Real ale, open fires, good food, accommodation, restaurant and car parking.
Facilities:	Room: ⅊✕👟🛏️📺 General: 🏠♨🚐✕✿

AXMINSTER

Kerrington House ★★★★★ Guest Accommodation

Musbury Road, Axminster, Devon, EX13 5JR   GOLD AWARD

T:	+44 (0) 1297 35333
E:	ja.reaney@kerringtonhouse.com
W:	kerringtonhouse.com
Bedrooms:	5 • sleeps 10
Prices:	Double: £50-£75 per person per night breakfast included Debit/credit card, cheques/cash accepted
Open:	Year round
Description:	Luxury, small hotel in impressive Victorian house in landscaped gardens. Furnished with elegance and style. Superb food, friendly informal service and attention to detail.
Facilities:	Room: ⅊✕📧👟✆🛏️📺 General: ⚷P♨✕✿🎌

AXMINSTER

Chuckle Too ★★★Self Catering

Chuckle Cottage, Main Street, Axminster TQ9 7BG

T:	+44 (0) 1803 712455
E:	jillyhanlon@beeb.net
W:	stay-in-devon.co.uk
Units:	1 • sleeps 3
Prices:	From £155-£397 per week
Open:	Year round
Description:	Chuckle Too, a modernised and completely self-contained wing of Chuckle Cottage, is fully-equipped, comfortable and pretty, sleeping up to three people, with double bed, sofa bed and a cot.
Facilities:	Room: 🛏 General: ♿♨ Leisure: ♪

BRENTOR

Burn Cottage ♦♦♦♦♦Guest Accommodation

West Blackdown, Brentor, Tavistock, Devon, PL19 0NB   SILVER AWARD

T:	+44 (0) 1822 820382
E:	welcome@burncottage.co.uk
W:	burncottage.co.uk
Bedrooms:	4 • sleeps 10
Prices:	Double: £30 per person per night breakfast included Debit/credit card accepted
Open:	Year round
Description:	Burn Cottage is in a location surrounded by the beauty of Dartmoor which can only be described as spiritually uplifting.
Facilities:	Room: 📺 General: **P**♿

BROADHEMBURY

Stafford Barton Farm ★★★★Farmhouse

Broadhembury, Honiton, Devon, EX14 3LU

T:	+44 (0) 1404 841403
E:	jean.walters1@tesco.net
Bedrooms:	2 • sleeps 4
Prices:	Double: £24-£30 per person per night breakfast included
Open:	Year round
Description:	Wonderful setting with views of the Blackdown Hills. Livestock enterprise on farm. Close to the picturesque village of Broadhembury.
Facilities:	Room: ✳♿ General: ♨♣

COLYTON

The Old Bakehouse   ♦♦♦♦ Guest Accommodation
Lower Church Street, Colyton, Devon, EX24 6ND

T:	+44 (0) 1297 552518
E:	sue.wiltshire@talk21.com
W:	theoldbakehousebandb.co.uk
Bedrooms:	5 • sleeps 10
Prices:	Double: £26-£35 per person per night breakfast included
Open:	Year round
Description:	A Grade II Listed 400-year-old former bakehouse recently restored; central but quiet location; en suite accommodation; guest lounge; restaurant (day and evening); tea garden.
Facilities:	Room: 🄵✖💧🛏️TV📶🍴 General: ✖P🛏️✖🌸🄴 Leisure: ♨️🐾🎣

COMBE MARTIN

Acorns Guesthouse   ★★★★ Guest Accommodation
2 Woodlands, Combe Martin, Devon, EX34 0AT

T:	+44 (0) 1271 882769
E:	info@acorns-guesthouse.co.uk
W:	acorns-guesthouse.co.uk
Bedrooms:	9 • sleeps 18
Prices:	Double: £45-£55 per room per night breakfast included Debit/credit card accepted
Open:	Year round
Description:	Our small, friendly licensed guesthouse is three minutes from the bay. Fully refurbished in 2002, all rooms are en suite.
Facilities:	Room: 🄵✖📺💧🛏️TV📶 General: P🛏️✖🌸🄴

CRANFORD

Cottages for the Connoisseur   ★★★★★ Self Catering
Penhaven Lodge, Rectory Lane, EX39 5PL

T:	+44 (0) 1237 451008
E:	reservations@connoisseur-cottages.co.uk
W:	connoisseur-cottages.co.uk
Units:	3 • sleeps 15
Prices:	From £399-£849 per week • Debit/credit card accepted
Open:	Year round
Description:	Delightful self-catering cottages, luxuriously equipped. Situated in quiet village with own woodland and nature trail. Ideally situated for RHS Rosemoor, Docton Mill and several other gardens and only a few miles from the coast.
Facilities:	General: P🛏️🌸📶

CRANFORD

Channel View ♦♦♦♦ Guest Accommodation

14 Teignmouth Hill, West Cliff, Dawlish, Devon, EX7 9DN

T:	+44 (0) 1626 866973
E:	channelviewguesthouse@fsmail.net
W:	channelviewguesthouse.co.uk
Bedrooms:	3 • sleeps 6
Prices:	Double: £22.50-£27.50 per person per night breakfast included • Euros accepted
Open:	Year round except Christmas and New Year
Description:	Our beautiful period house, which has lovely sea views from most rooms, has been upgraded to the highest standard and is only a few minutes' walk from the beach, lawn and stream as well as shops, railway and bus station.
Facilities:	Room: 📺 General: P

DULVERTON

Anstey Mills Cottages ★★★★ Self Catering

East Liscombe, Devon, TA22 9RZ

T:	+44 (0) 1398 341329
E:	ansteymills@yahoo.com
W:	ansteymillscottagedevon.co.uk
Units:	3 • sleeps 16
Prices:	From £195-£665 per week • Debit/credit card, euros accepted
Open:	Year round
Description:	Spacious barn conversion on Exmoor's border, a comfortable hideaway in peaceful, picturesque location. Good access to Devon's attractions and ideal for larger families.
Facilities:	General: P Leisure: ∪

EXETER

Exeter YHA ★★★ Hostel

47 Countess Wear Road, Exeter, Devon, EX2 6LR

T:	+44 (0) 1392 873329
E:	exeter@yha.org.uk
W:	yha.org.uk
Dormitories:	13 • sleeps 47
Prices:	Dormitory pricing: £8.50-£11.75 • Debit/credit card, cheques/cash accepted
Open:	Year round
Description:	Large house overlooking the River Exe on outskirts of ancient cathedral city, close to historic port of Topsham.
Facilities:	Room: 📺 General: P

EXETER

Telstar Hotel
★★★★ Guesthouse

75-77 St Davids Hill, Exeter, Devon, EX4 4DW

T:	+44 (0) 1392 272466
E:	reception@telstar-hotel.co.uk
W:	telstar-hotel.co.uk
Bedrooms:	20 • sleeps 37
Prices:	Double: £50-£65; Single: £27-£50; both per person per night breakfast included • Debit/credit card, cheques/cash accepted
Open:	Year round
Description:	A friendly, family-run B&B In a central position and near Exeter St David's railway station with parking.
Facilities:	Room: 🌡️✕⬛🔌☎💻📺🍵🛁 General: ✕🅿️🍴⚙️✕✂️🔌

GITTISHAM

Combe House Hotel & Restaurant
★★★ Hotel
GOLD AWARD

Gittisham, Honiton, Devon, EX14 3AD

T:	+44 (0) 1404 540400
E:	stay@thishotel.com
W:	thishotel.com
Bedrooms:	15 • sleeps 30
Prices:	Double: £148-£160 per room per night breakfast included Debit/credit card, cheques/cash accepted
Open:	Year round
Description:	Grade I Elizabethan manor house and restaurant in 3,500 acres of stunning park and woodland. One mile south-west of Honiton off A30. To Gittisham Village. Combe House is at the end of a mile of winding drive.
Facilities:	Room: ⬛🔌📠💻📺🍵🛁 General: 🅿️🍴⚙️👕✂️✕🔌 Leisure: ∪🚴🎣🐾

HORRABRIDGE

Brook House
◆◆◆◆◆ Guest Accommodation
GOLD AWARD

Horrabridge, Yelverton, Devon, PL20 7QT

T:	+44 (0) 1822 859225
E:	info@brook-house.com
W:	brook-house.com
Bedrooms:	3 • sleeps 6
Prices:	Double: £50 • Debit/credit card accepted
Open:	Year round
Description:	Located on Dartmoor near Tavistock. Victorian country house set in five acres. Luxury spacious en suite B&B accommodation.
Facilities:	Room: 🌡️✕⬛🔌💻📺🍵 General: ✕🅿️🍴👕✂️✕🔌

HORRABRIDGE

Overcombe Hotel   ★★★★ Guest Accommodation

Old Station Road, Horrabridge, Yelverton, Devon, PL20 7RA

T:	+44 (0) 1822 853501
E:	enquiries@overcombehotel.co.uk
W:	overcombehotel.co.uk
Bedrooms:	8 • sleeps 17
Prices:	Double: £50-£60 per room per night breakfast included; Single: £30-£40 per person per night breakfast included Debit/credit card accepted
Open:	Year round
Description:	Comfortable, fully en suite, non-smoking guest accommodation, situated within the Dartmoor National Park between Tavistock and Plymouth.
Facilities:	Room: 🕯✕⬜♿🛏📺📶 General: ✂P📶♟✕☼🔊 Leisure: 🚲

HUNTSHAM

Three Gates Farm   ★★★★ Self Catering

Huntsham, Tiverton, Devon, EX16 7QH

T:	+44 (0) 1398 331280
E:	threegatesfarm@hotmail.com
W:	threegatesfarm.co.uk
Units:	5 • sleeps up to 30
Prices:	From £150- £910 per week
Open:	Year round
Description:	Five self-catering cottages each sleeping two-six. Indoor pool, sauna, small fitness centre and games room. Set in 1.5 acres with pond and play area. Excellent base for exploring Devon.
Facilities:	General: P♿☼🔊📶🖥 Leisure: 🏊

ILFRACOMBE

St Brannocks House Hotel   ★★ Hotel

61 St Brannocks Road, Ilfracombe, Devon, EX34 8EQ

T:	+44 (0) 1271 863873
E:	stbrannocks@aol.com
W:	stbrannockshotel.co.uk
Bedrooms:	6 • sleeps 10
Prices:	Double or single room: £32 per person per night breakfast included • Debit/credit card, euros accepted
Open:	Year round except Christmas and New Year
Description:	Dog-friendly hotel situated in level position within walking distance of town and seafront. Licensed premises. Car parking for all.
Facilities:	Room: 🕯✕⬜♿🛏📺 General: P📶♟☼✕🔊 Leisure: ▶

ILFRACOMBE

The Ilfracombe Carlton Hotel ★★Hotel
Runnacleave Road, Ilfracombe, Devon, EX34 8AR

T:	+44 (0) 1271 862446
E:	enquiries@ilfracombecarlton.co.uk
W:	ilfracombecarlton.co.uk
Bedrooms:	48 • sleeps 95
Prices:	Double: £65-£70 per room per night breakfast included; Single: £32.50-£35 per person per night breakfast included Debit/credit card, cheques/cash accepted
Open:	Year round
Description:	Centrally situated hotel adjacent to National Trust walks, parks, theatre and seafront. Somewhere special for you.
Facilities:	Room: General:

LYNTON

Sinai House ◆◆◆◆ Guest Accommodation
Lynway, Lynton, Devon, EX35 6AY

T:	+44 (0) 1598 753227
E:	enquiries@sinaihouse.co.uk
W:	sinaihouse.co.uk
Bedrooms:	8 • sleeps 14
Prices:	Double: £24-£28; Single: £22-£26; both per person per night breakfast included • Debit/credit card, euros accepted
Open:	Year round except Christmas and New Year
Description:	An 1850 Victorian house offering magnificent sea views from en suite bedrooms and lounge in a peaceful atmosphere.
Facilities:	Room: General:

MORETONHAMPSTEAD

Budleigh Farm Self Catering rating applied for
Moretonhampstead, Newton Abbott, Devon, TQ13 8SB

T:	+44 (0) 1647 440835
E:	harvey@budleighfarm.co.uk
W:	budleighfarm.co.uk
Units:	7 • sleeps 22
Prices:	From £155-£515 per week • Debit/credit card, cheques/cash accepted
Open:	Year round
Description:	Seven barn conversions set at the end of a pretty valley, each with its own special character. Good all year.
Facilities:	General: Leisure:

OKEHAMPTON

East Hook Cottages
Self Catering rating applied for

West Hook Farm, Okehampton, Devon, EX20 1RL

T:	+44 (0) 1837 52305
E:	marystevens@westhookfarm.fsnet.co.uk
W:	easthook-holiday-cottages.co.uk
Units:	3 • sleeps 15
Prices:	From £140-£480 per week • Debit/credit card, euros accepted
Open:	Year round
Description:	Three real Devon country cottages with charm and ambiance and beautiful six mile panoramic view of Dartmoor. On Tarka Trail and cycleway 27.
Facilities:	General: P▦☒❄▯ Leisure: U☊⚓♪▸

PAIGNTON

Culverden Hotel
★★★Guest Accommodation

4 Colin Road, Paignton, Devon, TQ3 2NR

T:	+44 (0) 1803 559786
E:	info@culverdenhotel.co.uk
W:	culverdenhotel.co.uk
Bedrooms:	8 • sleeps 18
Prices:	Double and single: £18-£25 per person per night breakfast included • Debit/credit card accepted
Open:	Year round
Description:	Small, family-run, non-smoking guesthouse, 45 metres from the beach with en suite and family rooms, parking. A 10-minute level walk from town, bus and train.
Facilities:	Room: ▯✕☏TV General: ✗P☒▯

PANCRASWEEK

Tamarstone Farm
★★★Self Catering

Bude Road, Pancrasweek, Holsworthy, Devon, EX22 7JT

T:	+44 (0) 1288 381734
E:	cottage@tamarstone.co.uk
W:	tamarstone.co.uk
Units:	1 • sleeps 7
Prices:	From £240 • Cheques/cash accepted
Open:	Year round
Description:	Three-bed, centrally-heated cottage, sleeping seven. Peacefully situated on the Devon/Cornwall border. Ideal for touring both counties.
Facilities:	General: P☒❄▯ Leisure: ♪▸

PETROKSTOW

Off The Beaten Track   ★★★★Self Catering

Hallwood Farm, Petrokstow, Okehampton, EX20 3HP

T:	+44 (0) 1837 811762
E:	r.kelsey@farming.me.uk
W:	off-the-beaten-track.co.uk
Units:	1 • sleeps 10
Prices:	From £385-£930 per week • Debit/credit card, euros accepted
Open:	Year round
Description:	Beautifully situated farmhouse for 10 (four bedrooms/three bathrooms). Short walk to village pub/Tarka Trail. Facilities for cyclists and walkers include bike hire and 12-seat vehicle and bike trailer for excursions.
Facilities:	General: P⊠🏊🖳 Leisure: ᕔ🚲✿

PLYMOUTH

Imperial Hotel   ★★★Guest Accommodation

Lockyer Street, Plymouth, Devon, PL1 2QD

T:	+44 (0) 1752 227311
E:	neilimp@aol.com
W:	imperialplymouth.co.uk
Bedrooms:	20 • sleeps 43
Prices:	Double: £58; Single: £35-£46; both per room per night breakfast included • Debit/credit card, cheques/cash accepted
Open:	Year round
Description:	Personally run, owner-occupied, modernised Victorian hotel. Close to the Hoe, city centre. Car parking, restaurant.
Facilities:	Room: 📺🍵☎📺 General: 🛎⊠✕🍴

PYWORTHY

Leworthy Farmhouse   ★★★★Guest Accommodation

Pyworthy, Holsworthy, Devon,EX22 6SJ   SILVER AWARD

T:	+44 (0) 1409 259469
W:	leworthyfarmhouse.co.uk
Bedrooms:	7 • sleeps 18
Prices:	Double: £25 • Cheques/cash accepted
Open:	Year round
Description:	Georgian farmhouse nestling in tranquil backwater. Gardens, meadow, fishing lake. Chintzy curtains, chiming clocks, comfy old sofas, sparkling old china.
Facilities:	Room: 🛏✕📺🍵📺🕭 General: ✂🥾⊠✿🍴 Leisure: ♪

SEATON

Mariners Hotel ♦♦♦♦ Guest Accommodation
East Walk, Seaton, Devon, EX12 2NP

T:	+44 (0) 1297 20560
E:	mariners@aol.com
W:	marinershotelseaton.co.uk
Bedrooms:	10 • sleeps 19
Prices:	Double: £50-£60 per room per night breakfast included; Single: £25-£35 per person per night breakfast included
Open:	Year round except Christmas and New Year
Description:	Small, private hotel with 10 en suite bedrooms.
Facilities:	Room: ⁿ✕✿TV Ⅎ General: ⵁP⌨Ⅹ✕❉

SIDFORD

The Salty Monk ★★★★★ Restaurant with Rooms
Church Street, Sidford, Sidmouth, Devon, EX10 9QP   GOLD AWARD

T:	+44 (0) 1395 513174
E:	saltymonk@btconnect.com
W:	saltymonk.co.uk
Bedrooms:	5 • sleeps 10
Prices:	Double: £95 per room per night breakfast included. Debit/credit card, cheques/cash accepted
Open:	Year round
Description:	A 16thC award-winning restaurant complemented by five luxuriously appointed en suite rooms.
Facilities:	Room: ⁿ✕⌨✿⌨TV Ⅎ General: P⌨▲✕❉

SIDMOUTH

Cheriton Guesthouse ♦♦♦♦ Guest Accommodation
Vicarage Road, Sidmouth, Devon, EX10 8UQ

T:	+44 (0) 1395 513810
E:	sara.land1@virgin.net
W:	smoothhound.co.uk/hotels/cheritong.html
Bedrooms:	9 • sleeps 17
Prices:	Double and Single: £25-£30 per person per night breakfast included
Open:	Year round except Christmas and New Year
Description:	Cheriton, a large Victorian townhouse with nine comfortable en suite guest rooms, drink-making facilities and colour TV. All non-smoking.
Facilities:	Room: ⁿ✕✿⌨TV General: ⵁP✕❉

SOUTH ALLINGTON

South Allington House ★★★★ Guest Accommodation

South Allington, Chivelstone, Kingsbridge, Devon, TQ7 2NB

T:	+44 (0) 1548 511272
E:	barbara@sthallingtonbnb.demon.co.uk
W:	sthallingtonbnb.demon.co.uk
Bedrooms:	9 • sleeps 18
Prices:	Double: £60-£86 per room per night breakfast included; Single: £30 per person per night breakfast included Cheques/cash accepted
Open:	Year round
Description:	Attractive house set in four acres of beautiful gardens. Coastal walks leading to safe beaches, sailing, fishing, golf close at hand.
Facilities:	Room: ⁱ⁄✕◫➌☶▥.ⓉⓋ🔍 General: ⊱◫🐾✿🅗 Leisure: ⚲♪▸

STRETE

Strete Barton Farmhouse ★★★★ Guest Accommodation

Totnes Road, Strete, Dartmouth, Devon, TQ6 0RN   SILVER AWARD

T:	+44 (0) 1803 770364
E:	david@stretebarton.co.uk
W:	stretebarton.co.uk
Bedrooms:	6 • sleeps 12
Prices:	Double: £65-£85 per room per night breakfast included Debit/credit card, cheques/cash accepted
Open:	Year round
Description:	16thC farmhouse with stunning sea views. Six exquisitely furnished bedrooms either en suite or private facilities. English or Continental breakfast
Facilities:	Room: ⁱ⁄✕◫➌☶▥.ⓉⓋ◳🔍 General: P🐾✿🅗 Leisure: ▸

THELBRIDGE

Thelbridge Cross Inn   ♦♦♦♦ Guest Accommodation

Thelbridge, Crediton, Devon, EX17 4SQ

T:	+44 (0) 1884 860316
E:	admin@thelbridgexinn.co.uk
W:	westcountry-hotels.co.uk/thelbridgexinn
Bedrooms:	7 • sleeps 14
Prices:	Double: £20-£40 per person per night breakfast included Debit/credit card accepted
Open:	Year round
Description:	Peaceful, family-run country inn in the heart of rural Devon. Superb cuisine and comfortable surroundings and a relaxed, friendly atmosphere.
Facilities:	Room: ⁱ⁄✕◫➌🕯▥.ⓉⓋ🔍 General: ◫🅐🍴✕✿ Leisure: ℧▸

WEST BUCKLAND

Huxtable Farm   ♦♦♦♦ Guest Accommodation
West Buckland, Barnstaple, Devon, EX32 0SR   SILVER AWARD

T:	+44 (0) 1598 760254
E:	info@huxtablefarm.co.uk
W:	huxtablefarm.co.uk
Bedrooms:	6 • sleeps 16
Prices:	Double: £32-£45 per person per night breakfast included
	Debit/credit card/cheques/cash accepted
Open:	Year round except Christmas
Description:	Escape to this secluded, traditional Medieval farmhouse with quality en suite facilities, beams and log fires. Tennis court, sauna and wildlife trail. A Devon cream tea awaits you!
Facilities:	Room: 🏠✕⬛⬇🛏📺🕽
	General: 🗲P🐾✕☀🏛
	Leisure: ⚲⚑

ATHELHAMPTON

White Cottage   ★★★★B&B
White Cottage, Dorchester, Dorset, DT2 7LG   SILVER AWARD

T:	+44 (0) 1305 848622
E:	markjamespiper@aol.com
W:	webs.com/whitecottagebandb
Bedrooms:	2 • sleeps 4
Prices:	Double: £30-£35 per person per night breakfast included
Open:	Year round
Description:	A beautiful 300-year-old cottage, newly refurbished. Views over River Piddle and hills beyond, 200 yards from Athelhampton House.
Facilities:	Room: ⬛⬇🛏📺🕽
	General: 🗲P🐾☀🏛

BRIDPORT

At Home   ★★★★B&B
134 West Bay Road, Bridport, Dorset, DT6 4AZ

T:	+44 (0) 1308 458880
E:	dorset-coast@uk2.net
W:	dorset-coast.co.uk
Bedrooms:	3 • sleeps 6
Prices:	Double: £40-£65 per room per night breakfast included
	Debit/credit card accepted
Open:	Year round
Description:	Modern standard accommodation with a touch of luxury; friendly atmosphere; haven to Jurassic coastline and heritage site at West Bay and surrounding areas.
Facilities:	Room: 🏠✕⬛⬇🛏📺🕽
	General: 🗲P🐾

BRIDPORT

Smiths Farm Cottages ★★★Self Catering

Axminster Road, Charmouth, Bridport, Dorset, DT6 6BY

T:	+44 (0) 1297 560167
E:	smithscottages@btinternet.com
W:	eocities.com/smithsfarmcottages
Units:	2 • sleeps 9
Prices:	From £250-£695 per week
Open:	Year round
Description:	Barn conversion comprising of two semi-detached cottages in a lovely rural location with car parking.
Facilities:	General: P⚡☼▣

BROADOAK

Stoke Mill Farm ★★★Self Catering

Broadoak, Bridport, Dorset, DT6 5NR

T:	+44 (0) 1308 868036
W:	stokemillholidays.co.uk
Units:	6 • sleeps 20
Prices:	From £150-£425 per week • Cheques/cash accepted
Open:	Year round
Description:	Historic mill cottage, peaceful setting, beautiful countryside. Garden and patio. Ideal for walking, coast and National Trust land.
Facilities:	General: P⚡☼▣ Leisure: ∪

BROADWINDSOR

Crosskeys House ★★★★★B&B
SILVER AWARD

High Street, Broadwindsor, Beaminster, Dorset, DT8 3QP

T:	+44 (0) 1308 868063
E:	robin.ademey@care4free.net
Bedrooms:	2 • sleeps 4
Prices:	Double: £32.50-£40 • Debit/credit card, cheques/cash accepted
Open:	Year round
Description:	A warm welcome awaits at this historic village house. Very comfortable en suite bedrooms and lounge. Sumptuous breakfasts. Glorious countryside. Two double/twin rooms. Single rates also available.
Facilities:	Room: ⬚✖⬚⬚⬚,📺⬚ General: ✕⬚✖☼

CHARMOUTH

Knapp Cottages   ★★★★Self Catering

Booking: Lyme Bay Holidays, Boshouse, 44 Church Street, Lyme Regis DT7 3DA

T:	+44 (0) 1297 443363
E:	email@lymebayholidays.co.uk
W:	lymebayholidays.co.uk
Units:	1 • sleeps 4
Prices:	From £220 • Debit/credit card accepted
Open:	Year round
Description:	An attractive period cottage close to the village centre of Charmouth offering charm and character with the advantage of modern facilities.
Facilities:	General: ✂☼▤

CORSCOMBE

Rushbrook House   ★★★★B&B

Benville Lane, Benville, Nr Evershot, Dorchester, Dorset, DT2 0NN

T:	+44 (0) 1935 83244
E:	office@rushbrookhouse.co.uk
W:	rushbrookhouse.co.uk
Bedrooms:	2 • sleeps 4
Prices:	Double: £30-£34 per person per night breakfast included
Open:	Year round except Christmas and New Year
Description:	A large brick and flint two-storey house set in 4.75 acres of land in a quiet rural setting.
Facilities:	Call for details

FORDINGTON

Christmas Cottage   ★★★ Self Catering

12 Princes Street, Dorchester, Dorset, DT1 1TW

T:	+44 (0) 1305 264041
Units:	1 • sleeps 5
Prices:	From £175-£570 per week
Open:	Year round
Description:	Cottage in town centre and close to all amenities. Sleeps five. Ideal for visiting coast and country.
Facilities:	General: ✂▤

LYME REGIS

3 Dolphin Cottages   ★★★Self Catering

Booking: Sunnyside, Itchingfield, Horsham, RH13 0NX

T:	+44 (0) 1403 791258
Units:	1 • sleeps 4
Prices:	From £200 per week
Open:	Year round
Description:	Grade II Listed cottage. The Dolphin pub was converted to three cottages approximately 30 years ago. Close to shops and beach.
Facilities:	General: P✄▣

LYME REGIS

Bramcote Garden Apartment   ★★★★Self Catering

East Cliff, Lyme Regis, Dorset, DT7 3DH

T:	+44 (0) 1297 442924
E:	fnr.price@virgin.net
W:	bramcotelymeregis.com
Units:	2 • sleeps 4
Prices:	From £250 per week • Cheques/cash accepted
Open:	Year round except Christmas and New Year
Description:	Stylish refurbished garden apartment with patio overlooking the Heritage Coast. On-site parking, three minutes' walk to beach and town, coastal path five minutes away.
Facilities:	General: P✱▣ Leisure: ▶

MANSTON

Northwood Cottages   ★★★★Guest Accommodation

Manston, Sturminster Newton, Dorset, DT10 1HD   SILVER AWARD

T:	+44 (0) 1258 472666
E:	info@northwoodcottages.co.uk
W:	northwoodcottages.co.uk/affiliate/?id=visitbritainbnb
Bedrooms:	4 • sleeps 8
Prices:	Double and single: £29-£45 per person per night breakfast included • Debit/credit card, euros accepted
Open:	Year round
Description:	Luxury, heated en suite rooms recently renovated, beautiful rural Dorset farming area, full breakfast. Separate cosy lounge. Laundry, children welcome.
Facilities:	Room: ▨✕⬛✿▥.TV.☎ General: ✄P✄✕✿▤ Leisure: ∪♪▶

POOLE

Mariners Guesthouse ◆◆◆ Guest Accommodation

26 Sandbanks Road, Poole, BH14 8AQ

T:	+44 (0) 1202 247218
Bedrooms:	6 • sleeps 13
Prices:	Double or single room: £30 per person per night breakfast included • Cheques/cash accepted
Open:	Year round
Description:	A six-bedroomed guesthouse, B&B only. Close to seafront, ferry, civic centre, public park and town centre. Ideally situated for sailing, diving, windsurfing and cycling. We now use only organic produce, sourced locally.
Facilities:	Room: ⓢ✕⚓⛁🖥️ General: ✂P✗🚗✳️

PORTLAND

Portland Heights ★★★ Hotel

Yeates Corner, Portland, Dorset, DT5 2EN

T:	+44 (0) 1305 821361
E:	reception@portlandheights.co.uk
W:	portlandheights.co.uk
Bedrooms:	65 • sleeps 104
Prices:	Double: £34-72; Single: £68-£116; both per person per night breakfast included • Debit/credit card, cheques/cash accepted
Open:	Year round
Description:	Hotel situated on the summit of Portland in the centre of World Heritage Site, enjoying spectacular sea and coastal views. Leisure centre including pool, restaurant and bars.
Facilities:	Room: ⓢ✕🔌⚓🛁🖥️ General: ●P📱✗🚗✕🎵✳️ Leisure: ⚓U♨️♪❤

SHAFTSBURY

The Chalet ★★★★ B&B

SILVER AWARD

Christys Lane, Shaftesbury, Dorset, SP7 8DL

T:	+44 (0) 1747 853945
E:	enquiries@thechalet.biz
W:	thechalet.biz
Bedrooms:	2 • sleeps 4
Prices:	Double: £30-£40 per person per night breakfast included Euros accepted
Open:	Year round
Description:	Luxury accommodation in newly-built designer house. Fully equipped rooms. Choice of delicious breakfasts. Afternoon tea and cakes. Car park.
Facilities:	Room: ⓢ✕🔌⚓🛁🖥️ General: ✂✗✳️

SUTTON WALDRON

Vale Farm Holiday Cottages ★★★★ Self Catering
Vale Farm, Sutton Walden, Blandford Forum, Dorset, DT11 8PG

T:	+44 (0) 1747 811286
E:	valeholidays@tiscali.co.uk
W:	valeholidays.co.uk
Units:	2 • sleeps 8
Prices:	From £125-£550 per week
Open:	Year round
Description:	Luxury barn conversions in beautiful location tucked away on a picturesque dairy farm in rural Dorset. A warm welcome awaits.
Facilities:	General: P✄❄️🖳 Leisure: U♻️▸

WEYMOUTH

Chandlers Hotel ◆◆◆◆◆ Guest Accommodation
4 Westerhall Road, Weymouth, Dorset, DT4 7SZ   GOLD AWARD

T:	+44 (0) 1305 771341
E:	debbiesare@chandlershotel.com
W:	chandlershotel.com
Bedrooms:	9 • sleeps 17
Prices:	Double: £75-£120; Single: £40; both per room per night breakfast included • Debit/credit card accepted
Open:	Year round
Description:	The hotel is located 100 yards from seafront. Weymouth Sealife Centre and Lodmoor Country Park are approximately 800 metres. Weymouth town centre is a 10-minute walk along the seafront.
Facilities:	Room: ✖️📧✒️🍴📺🔧 General: P🎁💷✄❄️🖌️

WINTERBOURNE ABBAS

Lavender Lodge/The Granary ★★★ Self Catering
Booking: LGF Holidays, Little Glebe Farm, Winterbourne Abbas, DT2 9LS

T:	+44 (0) 1305 889662
E:	enquiries@lgf-holidays.co.uk
W:	lgf-holidays.co.uk
Units:	2 • sleeps 8
Prices:	From £185-£450 per week
Open:	Year round
Description:	Personally-run modern bungalow annexe offering direct access to footpaths through Hardy Country; pub five minutes' walk; relax and enjoy!
Facilities:	General: P✄❄️🖳

BARNARD CASTLE

Thorngate Coach House ★★★★Self Catering
Thorngate House, Thorngate, DL12 8PY

T:	+44 (0) 1833 637791
E:	info@thorngatecoachhouse.co.uk
W:	thorngatecoachhouse.co.uk
Units:	2 • sleeps 8
Prices:	From £225-£385 per week • Euros accepted
Open:	Year round
Description:	A converted 18thC coach house and stable buildings containing two self-catering units with a secluded courtyard for off-road secure parking.
Facilities:	General: P🅿️🌑🖥️ Leisure: 🎿U🐾♪►

CONSETT

Bee Cottage ★★★★Guesthouse
Bee Cottage Farm, Consett, Durham, DH8 9HW

T:	+44 (0) 1207 508224
E:	welcome@beecottagefarmhouse.freeserve.co.uk
W:	beecottage.co.uk
Bedrooms:	8 • sleeps 24
Prices:	Double: £32-£35 per room per night breakfast included Debit/credit card/cheques/cash accepted
Open:	Year round
Description:	Stunning views. Peaceful rural location between Tow Law and Castleside. All rooms en suite. Evening meals available. Licensed. Non-smoking. Ideal centre from which to explore the area.
Facilities:	Room: 🅱️✕📺🛁🖥️📺🖥️🗝️ General: ✂️🍽️🐾🚐✕🌑🍽️

CORNRIGGS

Cornriggs Cottages ★★★★Self Catering
c/o Low Cornriggs Farm DL13 1AQ

T:	+44 (0) 1388 537600
E:	enquiries@lowcornriggsfarm.fsnet.co.uk
W:	alstonandkillhoperidingcentre.co.uk
Units:	2 • sleeps 11
Prices:	From £250-£700 per week • Euros accepted
Open:	Year round
Description:	Two large, single-storey cottages. Three bedrooms, two bathrooms, well-fitted kitchen, lounge, patio, open view over Weardale.
Facilities:	General: P📺🌑🖥️🌑🖥️ Leisure: U🐾♪►

DURHAM

66 Claypath ★★B&B
66 Claypath, Durham, DH1 1QT

T:	+44 (0) 1913 843193
E:	richard@66claypath.co.uk
W:	66claypath.co.uk
Bedrooms:	2 • sleeps 3
Prices:	Double: £65; Single: £50; both per room per night breakfast included • Euros accepted
Open:	Year round
Description:	66 Claypath is a Listed Georgian house with a delightful secluded garden approximately four minutes' walk from Durham market square.
Facilities:	Room: ⬛✕⬛▥ⓉⓋ General: ✕⚕ Leisure: ▶

EDMUNDBYERS

Edmundbyers YHA ★★★Hostel
Edmundbyers, Consett, Durham, DH8 9NL

T:	+44 (0) 1207 255651
E:	edmundbyers@yha.org.uk
W:	yha.org.uk
Dormitories:	6 • sleeps 27
Prices:	Dormitory pricing: £8.95-£13 • Debit/credit card accepted
Open:	Year round except Christmas and New Year
Description:	Situated 0.5 miles from Derwent Reservoir. This hostel is a former inn dating from 1600 with beamed ceilings and is of historical interest.
Facilities:	Room: ⬛✕▥ General: ✕⬛⬛⬛▥⚡✳▥ Leisure: ⬛▶

FOREST IN TEESDALE

Langdon Beck YHA ★★★Hostel
Forest In Teesdale, Barnard Castle, Durham, DL12 0XN

T:	+44 (0) 1833 622228
E:	langdonbeck@yha.org.uk
W:	yha.org.uk
Dormitories:	8 • sleeps 20
Prices:	Dormitory pricing: £8.95 • Debit/credit card/cheques/cash accepted
Open:	Year round except Christmas and New Year
Description:	Comfortable youth hostel with family rooms, full catering service with residential license for beer and wine. The area is of special interest to botanists and geologists.
Facilities:	Room: ⬛✕⬛▥ⓉⓋ General: ✕P⬛▥⬛⬛✕⚡✳▥

HAMSTERLEY

Dale End
★★★★B&B

Hamsterley, Bishop Auckland, Durham, DL13 3PT
SILVER AWARD

T:	+44 (0) 1388 488091
E:	info@dale-endhamsterleybandb.co.uk
W:	dale-endhamsterleybandb.co.uk
Bedrooms:	2 • sleeps 5
Prices:	Double: £25-£30 per person per night breakfast included Euros accepted
Open:	Year round except Christmas and New Year
Description:	Dale End B&B offers en suite accommodation and ample parking, situated in a quiet cul-de-sac in the lovely rural village of Hamsterley. Secure storage and washing facilities available for cycles and motorcycles.
Facilities:	Room: 🔌📺 General: P Leisure:

HAMSTERLEY

Hamsterley B&B
★★★★B&B

Fern Lea, Hamsterley, Bishop Auckland, Durham, DL13 3PT   SILVER AWARD

T:	+44 (0) 1388 488056
Bedrooms:	2 • sleeps 4
Prices:	Double: £45 per room per night breakfast included Euros accepted
Open:	Year round except Christmas and New Year
Description:	Hamsterley B&B is fully equipped and furnished to the highest standards in a beautiful village near Raby Castle, Durham Cathedral and Hamsterley Forest.
Facilities:	Room: 🔌📺 General: P Leisure:

HUNDERTHWAITE

East Briscoe Farm Cottages
★★★★Self Catering

Baldersdale, Barnard Castle, Durham, DL12 9UL

T:	+44 (0) 1833 650087
E:	one@eastbriscoe.co.uk
W:	eastbriscoe.co.uk
Units:	6 • sleeps 20
Prices:	From £124 £469 • Debit/credit card/euros accepted
Open:	Year round except Christmas and New Year
Description:	Teesdale farm buildings converted to award-winning cottages. Beautiful estate with free river fishing and marked walks. Superb views of dale and moor.
Facilities:	General: P Leisure:

IRESHOPEBURN

Hillside Cottage   ★★★Self Catering
Booking: Hillside Cottage, 203 Fletton Avenue, Peterborough, PE2 8DE

T:	+44 (0) 1733 349612
E:	sasmc2000@yahoo.co.uk
W:	hillsidecottagedurham.co.uk
Units:	1 • sleeps 5
Prices:	From £180-£300 per week
Open:	Year round except Christmas and New Year
Description:	This two-bedroomed character cottage cut into the hillside beneath Ireshope Moor retains many original features and has panoramic views overlooking Weardale.
Facilities:	General: ✄❄🖵

LANEHEAD

Beckleshele   ★★★Self Catering
Blakeley Field, Lanehead, Bishop Auckland DL13 1AP

T:	+44 (0) 1388 537683
E:	ltaylor_blakeleyfield@yahoo.com
Units:	1 • sleeps 6
Prices:	From £295-£435 per week
Open:	Year round
Description:	One double with en suite shower, one twin and separate bathroom. Large kitchen/diner. Upstairs lounge with sofa bed. Magnificent views.
Facilities:	Room: 🛏 General: P✄❄❄🖵

MAINSFORTH

Swallow Cottage   ★★★★Self Catering
Mainsforth, Ferryhill, Durham, DL17 9AA

T:	+44 (0) 1740 656709
E:	maudes@onetel.net
W:	swallowcottage.visitnorthumbria.com
Units:	1 • sleeps 4
Prices:	From £180-£300 per week
Open:	Year round except Christmas and New Year
Description:	Four star farm cottage close to Durham City, sleeping four with lovely countryside views. Well equipped, children's playground, welcoming hosts.
Facilities:	Room: 🛏 General: ✄❄❄🗐🖵

MARWOOD

Hauxwell Grange Cottages ★★★★ Self Catering

Hauxwell Grange, Barnard Castle, Durham, DL12 8QU

T:	+44 (0) 1833 695022
E:	hauxwellvmp@supaworld.com
W:	hauxwellgrangecottages.co.uk
Units:	2 • sleeps 6
Prices:	From £170-£350 per week • Cheques/cash accepted
Open:	Year round except Christmas and New Year
Description:	The Stone Byre sleeps four (plus cot) and Curlew Cottage sleeps two. Two cosy well-equipped stone cottages, set in the beautiful open countryside of unspoilt Teesdale.
Facilities:	Room: ▥ General: P✗♿❄☐ Leisure: U♿♪↟

MIDDLETON-IN-TEESDALE

Brunswick House ★★★★ Guesthouse

55 Market Place, Barnard Castle, Durham, DL12 0QH SILVER AWARD

T:	+44 (0) 1833 640393
E:	enquiries@brunswickhouse.net
W:	brunswickhouse.net
Bedrooms:	5 • sleeps 10
Prices:	Double: £26-£29 per person per night breakfast included Debit/credit card, cheques/cash accepted
Open:	Year round except Christmas
Description:	Comfortable 18thC stone-built guesthouse, overlooking village green, with a reputation for good home cooking and friendly service. Tastefully restored and decorated retaining much character and many original features.
Facilities:	Room: ↡✗⬚♨♥▥.TV▥☎ General: ✂P◨♨♿♣✗❄▥

QUEBEC

Hamsteels Hall ★★★★ Farmhouse

Hamsteels Lane, Quebec, Durham, DH7 9RS

T:	+44 (0) 1207 520388
E:	june@hamsteelshall.co.uk
W:	hamsteelshall.co.uk
Bedrooms:	5 • sleeps 12
Prices:	Double: £20-£25 per person per night breakfast included Cheques/cash accepted
Open:	Year round except Christmas and New Year
Description:	Serviced accommodation in an historical building with four-poster beds, en suite facilities and panoramic views. Ideal for country walks, cycling or touring. Only 10 minutes' drive from Durham City; 15 minutes' from Beamish.
Facilities:	Room: ↡✗⬚♨♥▥.TV▥☎ General: ✂P♣♿♣❄▥ Leisure: U

TRIMDON GRANGE

Polemonium Plantery ★★★★ B&B

28 Sunnyside Terrace, Trimdon Station, Durham, TS29 6HF

T:	+44 (0) 1429 881529
E:	bandb@polemonium.co.uk
W:	polemonium.co.uk
Bedrooms:	3 • sleeps 4
Prices:	Double: £45-£60; Single: £20-£24.99 both per room per night breakfast included
Open:	Year round
Description:	A peaceful retreat in a small country village with good access to coast and country.
Facilities:	Room: ⚙️✖️☎️🛏️🖥️📺📻 General: ✂️💺🅰️✖️❄️ Leisure: 🚲

WINSTON

The Cottage at Alwent Mill ★★★★ Self Catering

Alwent Mill DL2 3QH

T:	+44 (0) 1325 730479
E:	libby@alwentmill.co.uk
Units:	1 • sleeps 4
Prices:	From £420 per week
Open:	Year round except Christmas and New Year
Description:	A fabulous 'home from home' holiday cottage sleeping four, set in beautiful unspoilt countryside, along the banks of Alwent Beck.
Facilities:	Call for details

WOLSINGHAM

Whitfield House Cottage ★★★ Self Catering

Booking: Whitfield House Cottage, 25 Front Street, Wolsingham, DL13 3DF

T:	+44 (0) 1388 527466
E:	enquiries@whitfieldhouse.clara.net
W:	whitfieldhouse.clara.net
Units:	1 • sleeps 7
Prices:	From £195-£420 per week • Euros accepted
Open:	Year round except Christmas and New Year
Description:	Spacious accommodation in part of an attractive Queen Anne period house. Near the centre of this small former market town which is situated in Weardale, one of the North Pennine Dales.
Facilities:	General: P💺❄️🖥️

WYCLIFFE

Boot and Shoe Cottage ★★★★Self Catering

Booking: Waterside Cottage, Wycliffe, Barnard Castle, DL12 9TR

T:	+44 (0) 1833 627200
E:	info@bootandshoecottage.co.uk
W:	bootandshoecottage.co.uk
Units:	1 • sleeps 4
Prices:	From £295-£380 per week • Cheques/cash accepted
Open:	Year round
Description:	An idyllic cottage overlooking River Tees. Recently restored and with all 'mod cons', log fire etc. Private fishing.
Facilities:	Room: 🛏 General: P🅿🛗🚭🐾☎📱 Leisure: 🎣

LAMARSH

Hill Farm House ★★★★Self Catering

Hill Farm House, Lamarsh, Bures, Essex, CO8 5HB

T:	+44 (0) 1787 269905
E:	greenhillaccom@tiscali.co.uk
W:	farmstayeastanglia.co.uk
Units:	1 • sleeps 2
Prices:	From £252 per week
Open:	Year round
Description:	Quality self-catering apartment on Essex/Suffolk border near, Sudbury. Tel +44 (0) 1787 269905 for brochure.
Facilities:	General: ✿

RADWINTER

Little Bulls Farmhouse ★★★★Self Catering

Radwinter Park, Saffron Walden, Essex CB10 2UE

T:	+44 (0) 1799 599272
E:	ajkiddy@cambridge-vacation-homes.com
W:	cambridge-vacation-homes.com
Units:	1 • sleeps 9
Prices:	From £413 per week
Open:	Year round
Description:	Little Bulls Farmhouse located on a private farm bordering South Cambridgeshire and North Essex. Recently renovated, fitted and furnished to four stars.
Facilities:	General: ✿

STEEPLE

The Star Inn ♦♦♦♦ Guest Accommodation

The Street, Steeple, Southminster, Essex, CM0 7LF

T:	+44 (0) 1621 772646
Bedrooms:	4 • sleeps 9
Prices:	Double: £40-£55 per room per night breakfast included Debit/credit card, cheques/cash accepted
Open:	Year round except Christmas and New Year
Description:	The Star is a family-run pub providing modern accommodation and home-cooked food. Caravan hook-ups also available.
Facilities:	Room: ⚄✕📺♨🛏📺🔌 General: P🏧⚓✗✖❄

BLOCKLEY

Honeysuckle Cottage ★★★★Self Catering

Booking address:13 Serpentine Road, Harborne, Birmingham, B17 9RD

T:	+44 (0) 121 426 6310
E:	stjohn.daly@blueyonder.co.uk
W:	thecountrycottage.co.uk
Units:	1 • sleeps 3
Prices:	From £245 per week
Open:	Year round
Description:	Charming Grade II Listed stone cottage set in beautiful Cotswold village. Has a wealth of character including beamed ceilings, internal stone walls and wood-burning stove.
Facilities:	General: ✗❄🔌 Leisure: U♞🎣🏇

BULLO PILL

Grove Farm ★★★★Farmhouse

Bullo Pill, Newnham, Gloucestershire, GL14 1DZ

T:	+44 (0) 1594 516304
E:	davidandpennyhill@btopenworld.com
W:	grovefarm-uk.com
Bedrooms:	2 • sleeps 4
Prices:	Double: £30-£35 per person per night breakfast included
Open:	Year round
Description:	Traditional farmhouse an organic dairy farm, with panoramic views over River Severn Estuary towards the Cotswolds.
Facilities:	Room: 📺♨📺🔌 General: ⚓✗❄🍴 Leisure: U♞

KINGS STANLEY

Valley Views ★★★★ Guest Accommodation

12 Orchard Close, Kings Stanley, Stonehoue, Gloucestershire, GL10 3QA

T:	+44 (0) 1453 827458
W:	valley-views.com
Bedrooms:	3 • sleeps 6
Prices:	Double: £56-£70 per room per night breakfast included
Open:	Year round
Description:	Situated in Kings Stanley on the Cotswold Way and set in landscaped gardens with breathtaking Cotswold views. Recently refurbished chalet style bungalow. Excellent touring base. Extensive home-cooked menu.
Facilities:	Room: ⬛✕⬛⬛⬛📺🔌 General: ✕⬛✕⬛⬛

RENDCOMB

Landage House ◆◆◆◆ Guest Accommodation

Rendcomb, Cirencester, Gloucestershire, GL7 7HB

T:	+44 (0) 1285 831250
E:	carol.landage@amserve.com
Bedrooms:	3 • sleeps 6
Prices:	Double: £55-65per room per night breakfast included Cheques/cash accepted
Open:	Year round
Description:	Superb, small, manor-type house. Very warm and comfortable, quiet at night. Excellent walks, glorious views. Outdoor, heated pool.
Facilities:	Room: ⬛⬛⬛⬛🔌 General: ⬛⬛⬛ Leisure: ⬛⬛

ST CATHERINE

Nailey Cottages ★★★★ Self Catering

Nailey Farm, St Catherine's Valley, Bath, BA1 8HD

T:	+44 (0) 1225 852989
E:	cottages@naileyfarm.co.uk
W:	naileyfarm.co.uk
Units:	3 • sleeps 16
Prices:	From £300-£850 per week • Debit/credit card, cheques/cash accepted
Open:	Year round
Description:	Idyllic farm retreat in dramatic valley on Cotswold edge. Area of outstanding natural beauty. Abundant wildlife, ideal walking. Imaginative conversion. Highly desirable interiors. All comforts.
Facilities:	General: P⬛⬛⬛⬛⬛

STOW ON THE WOLD

South Hill Farmhouse ★★★★ Guest Accommodation
Station Road, Stow on the Wold, Cheltenham, Gloucestershire, GL54 1JU

T:	+44 (0) 1451 831888
E:	info@southhill.co.uk
W:	southhill.co.uk
Bedrooms:	6 • sleeps 16
Prices:	Double: £50-55 per room per night breakfast included Debit/credit card, cheques/cash accepted
Open:	Year round
Description:	A traditional family-run B&B providing a warm welcome and an excellent base in the heart of the Cotswolds.
Facilities:	Room: ♨✕⬛♨▥.TV General: ⚡P⬛✂❋ Leisure: ∪

STOW ON THE WOLD

YHA Stow-on-the-Wold ★★★★ Hostel
The Square, Cheltenham, Gloucestershire, GL54 1AF

T:	+44 (0) 1451 830497
E:	stow@yha.org.uk
W:	yha.org.uk
Dormitories:	9 • sleeps 43
Prices:	Dormitory pricing: £9.50-£13.75 • Debit/credit card, cheques/cash accepted
Open:	Year round except Christmas
Description:	A 16thC building in historic market square. Has recently been refurbished thanks to a Heritage Lottery Fund grant.
Facilities:	Room: ♨✕▥.TV General: ⚡P⬛✂🖶✕⬛

TEWKESBURY

9 Mill Bank ★★ Self Catering
Booking address: 7 Mill Bank, Tewkesbury, Gloucestershire, GL20 5SD

T:	+44 (0) 1684 276190
E:	billhunt@9mb.co.uk
W:	tewkesbury-cottage.co.uk
Units:	1 • sleeps 2
Prices:	From £250-350 per week • Euros accepted
Open:	Year round
Description:	A 16thC Grade II Listed, bijou, riverside cottage, in delightful medieval town. Original features, outstanding views and unique "olde worlde" charm. Single night rates available from £50 per night.
Facilities:	General: ✂⬛ Leisure: ♪↑

WILLERSEY

3 Cheltenham Cottages ★★Self Catering
Booking address: 28 Bibsworth Avenue, Broadway, WR12 7BQ

T:	+44 (0) 1386 853248
E:	g.malin@virgin.net
Units:	1 • sleeps 3
Prices:	From £185 per week
Open:	Year round
Description:	Grade II Listed Cotswold stone cottage, countryside views. Award-winning village, excellent shop and pubs. Ideal for exploring Cotswold and Shakespeare country.
Facilities:	General: ✂✿🖵 Leisure: ♈

GREENFIELD

Clifton Cottage ★★★Self-Catering/Serviced Apartments
111 Chew Valley Road, Greenfield, Oldham, OL3 7JJ

T:	+44 (0) 1457 872098
E:	ced117@aol.com
W:	tarter.easily.co.uk/users/www.saddleworth-vacations.co.uk/index.php
Units:	1 • sleeps 5
Prices:	From £250-£300 per week
Open:	Year round
Description:	Cosy country cottage
Facilities:	General: 🛏✂🖵

HIGH LANE

Ty Coch ★★★★Self Catering
31 Cromley Road, High Lane, Stockport, SK6 8BU

T:	+44 (0) 1457 872098
Units:	1 • sleeps 4-6
Prices:	From £250-£280 per week
Open:	Year round except Christmas and New Year
Description:	This two-bedroomed bungalow sleeps four-six people. The kitchen has all facilities with TVs in the lounge and bedrooms.
Facilities:	Room: 📺

ROCHDALE

Fernhill Barn B&B ◆◆◆◆Guest Accommodation

Fernhill Lane, Lanehead, Rochdale, OL12 6BW

T:	+44 (0) 1706 355671
E:	info@fernhillbarn.com
W:	fernhillbarn.com
Bedrooms:	8 • sleeps 17
Prices:	Double: £39.95; Single: £27.50; both per room per night room only • Debit/credit card accepted
Open:	Year round
Description:	16thC stone barn conversion.
Facilities:	Room: ⚒✕⊡⚘ⅢⅢ.TV⊟⚏⚘ General: ✕P⊞⚒⚷⚔↰✕⚘ Leisure: ▶

BENTLEY

Green Farm ★★★★Self Catering

The Drift, Bentley, Farnham, GU10 5JX

T:	+44 (0) 1420 23246
E:	chris@powellmessenger.co.uk
W:	greenfarm.org.uk
Units:	1 • sleeps 5
Prices:	From £245-£525 per week • Euros accepted
Open:	Year round
Description:	Luxury, self-contained accommodation in newly-built annexe of Listed farmhouse. Fully fitted and very spacious. Terrace and ample parking. Full details on website.
Facilities:	General: P⚷⚘⚏ Leisure: ⚲

BURLEY

Wayside Cottage ★★★★B&B

27 Garden Road, Burley, Ringwood, Hampshire, BH24 4EA

T:	+44 (0) 1425 403414
E:	jwest@wayside-cottage.co.uk
W:	wayside-cottage.co.uk
Bedrooms:	6 • sleeps 14
Prices:	Double: £25-£30 per person per night breakfast included
	Cheques/cash accepted
Open:	Year round
Description:	An Edwardian cottage in the New Forest where ponies, donkeys and even cattle wander down the streets. A perfect haven for a relaxing weekend, or a longer stay. Cycling, walking and horse riding are within five minutes' walk.
Facilities:	Room: ⚒✕Ⅲ.TV General: ✕PX⚘⚔ Leisure: U▶

65

IBTHORPE

Staggs Cottage ★★★★B&B

Windmill Hill, Ibthorpe, Andover, Hampshire, SP11 0BP

T:	+44 (0) 1264 736235
E:	staggscottage@aol.com
W:	staggscottage.co.uk
Bedrooms:	3 • sleeps 6
Prices:	Double £27.50 per person per night breakfast included
Open:	Year round except Christmas and New Year
Description:	Staggs Cottage is in peaceful countryside, on the Test Way, with magnificent views over the Bourne Valley. Double- and twin-bedded rooms sharing a bath/shower. Twin room with private shower. Tea-/coffee-making facilities in all.
Facilities:	Room: 🍵📺 General: ❄️🏛

LINWOOD

High Corner Inn ♦♦♦Guest Accommodation

Linwood, Ringwood, Hampshire, BH24 3QY

T:	+44 (0) 1425 473973
Bedrooms:	7 • sleeps 16
Prices:	Double: £50-£120 per room per night breakfast included Debit/credit, cheques/cash accepted
Open:	Year round
Description:	In the heart of the New Forest, seven quality en suite letting rooms, log fires, large garden, pet friendly.
Facilities:	Room: 🍵👤📶📺🍵 General: P🏛🍷🎵❄️🐾 Leisure: ∪🏇

LYNDHURST

Bay Tree Cottage ★★★★Self Catering

12 Princes Crescent, Lyndhurst, Hampshire, SO43 7BS

T:	+44 (0) 23 8028 2821
Units:	1 • sleeps 5
Prices:	From £300-£690 per week • Debit/credit card accepted
Open:	Year round
Description:	Delightful, well-equipped cottage close to Lyndhurst Village centre. Sitting room, separate dining room, kitchen, cloakroom, three bedrooms, bathroom and garden.
Facilities:	General: P❄️📱

LYNDHURST

Clayhill House ♦♦♦♦ Guest Accommodation
Clay Hill, Lyndhurst, Hampshire, SO43 7DE

T:	+44 (0) 23 8028 2304
E:	clayhillhouse@tinyworld.co.uk
W:	clayhillhouse.co.uk
Bedrooms:	3 • sleeps 8
Prices:	Double: £27 per person per night breakfast included Debit/credit card accepted
Open:	Year round
Description:	Built in 1830, this former country house offers all rooms en suite, plus a drying room for ramblers and cyclists.
Facilities:	Room: ▥ General: ⚡P▣⌗ Leisure: ▶

WINCHESTER

87 Christchurch Road ★★★★ Self Catering
87 Christchurch Road, Winchester, Hampshire, SO23 9QY

T:	+44 (0) 1962 854902
E:	liz@peacocke.wanadoo.co.uk
W:	cottageguide.co.uk
Units:	2 • sleeps 6
Prices:	From £450 per week • Euros accepted
Open:	Year round except Christmas and New Year
Description:	Self-contained, two double-bedroomed apartment on second floor of Victorian House. Own entrance, long views towards St Catherine's Hill.
Facilities:	General: P⌗✾⌂

AVENBURY

The Old Cowshed ♦♦♦♦ Guest Accommodation
Avenbury, Bromyard, Herefordshire, HR7 4LA

T:	+44 (0) 1885 482384
E:	combes@cowshed.uk.com
W:	cowshed.uk.com
Bedrooms:	3 • sleeps 6
Prices:	Double: £26-£32 per person per night breakfast included Debit/credit card accepted
Open:	Year round
Description:	B&B in Listed, converted farm buildings, ground floor rooms, with inglenook fireplace in lounge. Car park and gardens in peaceful, countryside location. Dinner available.
Facilities:	Room: ▦✕▯▤▥.⟁⌐ General: ⚡▲✕✾▤

BREDWARD

Cider Press Cottage ★★★★ Self Catering

Bredward Farm, Kington, HR5 3HP

T:	+44 (0) 1544 231462
Units:	1 • sleeps 4
Prices:	From £204-£411 per week
Open:	Year round
Description:	Restored and beautifully presented, Cider Press Cottage is attached to the owners' 16thC farmhouse on their working sheep and beef farm. Stunning views are offered across the valleys and towards the owners' landscaped lake.
Facilities:	General: ☒❀▣

DORSTONE

Cottage Farm ♦♦♦ Guest Accommodation

Middlewood, Hereford, HR3 5SX

T:	+44 (0) 1497 831496
E:	julie@hgjmjones.freeserve.co.uk
W:	smoothhound.co.uk/hotels/cottagef.html
Bedrooms:	2 • sleeps 4
Prices:	Double: £20 per person per night breakfast included Cheques/cash accepted
Open:	Year round
Description:	Ground floor rooms in a peaceful, comfortable home at the head of the Golden and Wye Valley. Also awarded the Green Tourism Award.
Facilities:	Room: ▦✕▣▮◖▥回尽 General: ⊬☒✕❀ Leisure: ∪♪▶

FOWNHOPE

Birds Farm Cottage ★★★ Self Catering

White House, How Caple, Hereford, HR1 4SR

T:	+44 (0) 1989 740644
E:	birdscottage@yahoo.com
Units:	1 • sleeps 4
Prices:	From £150-£1,200 per week • Cheques/cash accepted
Open:	Year round
Description:	Birds Farm Cottage is very popular with people who enjoy the peace and tranquillity of the countryside. Whether they want to walk or just sit in the gardens and observe the many different birds and wildlife around.
Facilities:	General: P▣☒❀▣ Leisure: ∪☙✿♪⟡

HOW CAPLE

The Falcon   ◆◆◆◆Guest Accommodation

How Caple, Hereford, HR1 4TF

T:	+44 (0) 1989 740223
E:	falconguesthouse@tinyworld.co.uk
Bedrooms:	4 • sleeps 9
Prices:	Double: £19.50 per person per night breakfast included
Open:	Year round
Description:	Grade II Listed, Georgian house set in pleasant pasture land, near to beautiful Wye Valley and easy access to Hereford, Ross-on-Wye and M50.
Facilities:	Room: ⁵✕🛁🛏📺 General: ✕🏫🅿✕❄

LEINTWARDINE

Mocktree Barns Holiday Cottages ★★★Self Catering

Leintwardine, Ludlow, SY7 0LY

T:	+44 (0) 1547 540441
E:	mocktreebarns@care4free.net
W:	mocktreeholidays.co.uk
Units:	5 • sleeps 12
Prices:	From £195-£375 per week
Open:	Year round
Description:	Comfortable, well-equipped character cottages round sunny courtyard. Friendly welcome, gardens, delightful views. Ideal walking, cycling, wildlife, touring. Ludlow six miles. No smoking. Pets and children welcome.
Facilities:	Room: ⁵✕ General: ✕🅿❄✕🐕🖥🖥

MADLEY

Shenmore Cottage B&B ★★★★Guest Accommodation

Upper Shenmore, Madley, Hereford, HR2 9NX

T:	+44 (0) 1981 250507
E:	shenmorecottage@aol.com
W:	bedandbreakfast-herefordshire.com
Bedrooms:	2 • sleeps 4
Prices:	Double: £25per person per night breakfast included Euros accepted
Open:	Year round
Description:	Recently refurbished Victorian Cottage in Herefordshire countryside. All rooms en suite, non-smoking home. Aga-cooked breakfasts, a warm welcome awaits.
Facilities:	Room: ⁵✕🔌🛁🛏📺 General: ✕✂✕

MUCH COWARNE

Cowarne Hall Cottages ★★★★Self Catering

Much Cowarne, Bromyard, HR7 4JQ

T:	+44 (0) 1432 820317
E:	rm@cowarnehall.co.uk
W:	cowarnehall.co.uk
Units:	4 • sleeps 8
Prices:	From £180-£410 per week • Euros accepted
Open:	Year round
Description:	Historic cottages with pretty gardens and wonderful views. Rural and peaceful, yet convenient for Malvern, Hereford, Worcester and the Wye Valley.
Facilities:	General: P(目⊠❉回☐ Leisure: ∪⅋♪⊩

RICHARDS CASTLE

Stables Flat ★★★★Self Catering

Woodhouse Farm, Richards Castle, Ludlow, SY8 4EU

♫	+44 (0) 1584 831265
Units:	1 • sleeps 2
Prices:	From £160-£250 per week
Open:	Year round except Christmas and New Year
Description:	Spacious upstairs, beamed stables flat, comfortably fitted, linen and towels provided, overlooking attractive garden glorious views, ideal base cycling, walking, bird watching, touring, also short breaks.
Facilities:	General: P⊠❉回☐

WHITCHURCH

Norton Cottages ★★★★Self Catering

Norton House, Whitchurch, Ross on Wye, HR9 6DJ

T:	+44 (0) 1600 890046
E:	enquiries@norton.wyenet.co.uk
W:	norton-cottages.com
Units:	2 • sleeps 4
Prices:	From £250-£385 per week • Cheques/cash accepted
Open:	Year round
Description:	Two very individual cottages, tastefully created from a 16thC Listed building. Catering for two adults, dog friendly, contained gardens.
Facilities:	General: P❉⊩回☐

WILTON

Benhall Farm
♦♦♦♦ Guest Accommodation

Wilton, Ross-on-Wye, HR9 6AG — SILVER AWARD

T:	+44 (0) 1989 563900
E:	info@benhallfarm.co.uk
W:	benhallfarm.co.uk
Bedrooms:	3 • sleeps 8
Prices:	Double: £25-28 per person per night breakfast included Debit/credit card accepted
Open:	Year round
Description:	Enjoy the splendour of our Georgian farmhouse with wonderful views, spacious rooms and wholesome varied breakfasts from local produce where available. Walking, wildlife, cycling, golf, fishing are all with easy access.
Facilities:	Room: ⓑ✕⬛♨🛁🖥📺📶 General: ⼁♨⌖🅿 Leisure: ⟋⬥▸

BINSTEAD

Sillwood Acre
♦♦♦♦ Guest Accommodation

Church Road, Binstead, Binstead, PO33 3TB — SILVER AWARD

T:	+44 (0) 1983 563553
E:	debbie@sillwood-acre.co.uk
W:	sillwood-acre.co.uk
Bedrooms:	3 • sleeps 6
Prices:	Double: £25-£33per person per night breakfast included
Open:	Year round except Christmas and New Year
Description:	Sillwood Acre is a large Victorian house, built in 1856 and set in one acre of informal gardens. Open for B&B since 1994, offering large, comfortable rooms and a relaxed, quiet, friendly atmosphere. There is ample off-road car parking. Binstead is on the outskirts of Ryde just a few minutes by car from the Portsmouth-Fishbourne car ferry terminal.
Facilities:	Room: ⬛♨📺📶 General: ⼁🅿⌖

FRESHWATER

Rockstone Cottage
♦♦♦♦ Guest Accommodation

Colwell Chine Road, Colwell Bay, Freshwater, PO40 9NR

T:	+44 (0) 1983 753723
E:	nicky.drew@btopenworld.com
W:	rockstonecottage.co.uk
Bedrooms:	5 • sleeps 11
Prices:	Double: £26 per person per night breakfast included
Open:	Year round except Christmas and New Year
Description:	A charming cottage built in 1790, situated 300 yards from Colwell Bay and its safe, sandy beach. Surrounded by lovely walks and picturesque countryside, riding stables, golf and leisure centre nearby.
Facilities:	Room: ⬛♨📺📶 General: ⼁⬛⌖🅿 Leisure: ∪▸

GODSHILL

Lake View ★★★★Self Catering

Godshill Park Farm House, Shanklin Road, Ventnor, PO38 3JF

T:	+44 (0) 1983 753723
W:	godshillparkfarm.uk.com
Units:	1 • sleeps 6
Prices:	From £250-£749 per week
Open:	Year round except Christmas and New Year
Description:	This newly furbished wing of the house provides spacious accommodation all on one level. Accommodating six people. The south-facing terrace looks out over the garden to the millpond and the woods and farmland beyond.
Facilities:	Room: 🗙 General: 📶🖥 Leisure: ∪🌙

NEWPORT

Litten Park Guesthouse ♦♦♦♦Guest Accommodation

48 Medina Avenue, Newport, PO30 1EL

T:	+44 (0) 1983 526836
Bedrooms:	5 • sleeps 8
Prices:	Double: £24; Single: £27.50-29.50; both per person per night breakfast included
Open:	Year round except Christmas and New Year
Description:	Small, homely guesthouse, within easy walking distance of main island town of Newport. On site parking.
Facilities:	Room: 🕯📺 General: ✂P❄

SANDOWN

Chad Hill Hotel ★★ Small Hotel

7 Hill Street, Sandown, PO36 9DD

T:	+44 (0) 1983 403231
E:	enquiries@chadhillhotel.co.uk
W:	chadhillhotel.co.uk
Bedrooms:	14 • sleeps 37
Prices:	Double and single: £24-£29 per person per night breakfast included
Open:	Year round except Christmas and New Year
Description:	A beautiful, Victorian house built in the 1850s with a history linked to Queen Victoria's family. In a quiet area and a short walk from Sandown with its beach, pier and traditional seaside entertainment. Sandown also has an 18-hole golf course plus pitch and putt.
Facilities:	Room: 🕯🗙📧🕯📞🛗📺🗣 General: 📞🗙❄🗡 Leisure: ▶

SANDOWN

Haytor Lodge　　　　◆◆◆◆ Guest Accommodation
16 Cliff Path, Lake, PO36 8PL

T:	+44 (0) 1983 402969
Bedrooms:	6 • sleeps 19
Prices:	Double: £18 per person per night breakfast included
Open:	Year round except Christmas and New Year
Description:	Contact lodge for details.
Facilities:	Room: ⚲TV General: ▥✕☼🏳

SANDOWN

Sandhill Hotel　　　　◆◆◆◆ Guest Accommodation
6 Hill Street, Sandown, PO36 9DB

T:	+44 (0) 1983 403635
E:	sandhillhotel@btconnect.com
W:	sandhill-hotel.com
Bedrooms:	16 • sleeps 45
Prices:	Double and single: £26 per person per night breakfast included Debit/credit card, euros accepted
Open:	Year round except Christmas and New Year
Description:	A spacious hotel in a pleasant residential area of Sandown. The beach, town centre and railway station are all within easy walking distance. The hotel offers the comforts and facilities to let guests of all ages enjoy their holiday in a friendly and relaxing atmosphere.
Facilities:	Room: ✕▣⚲📞TV♨ General: ✂▥☒🏤✕☼🏳 Leisure: ♻

SHANKLIN

Atholl Court　　　　★★★ Guesthouse
1 Atherley Road, Shanklin, PO37 7AT

T:	+44 (0) 1983 862414
E:	info@atholl-court.co.uk
W:	atholl-court.co.uk
Bedrooms:	8 • sleeps 13
Prices:	Double: £23.50-£26.50; Single: £22.50-25.50; both per person per night breakfast included • Debit/credit card accepted
Open:	Year round except Christmas and New Year
Description:	This peaceful guesthouse, has warm comfortable rooms. Close to bus station, shops and beach and within 100 yards of the train station. Own car park.
Facilities:	Room: ⚲TV General: ✂P▥

SHANKLIN

Sherwood Court Hotel ★★Hotel
Atherley Road, Shanklin, PO37 7AU

T:	+44 (0) 1983 862518
E:	enquiries@sherwoodcourthotel.com
W:	sherwoodcourthotel.com
Bedrooms:	52 • sleeps 106
Prices:	Double: £40 per person per night breakfast included Debit/credit card accepted
Open:	Year round except Christmas and New Year
Description:	Near to both the beach and the bustling town of Shanklin and the many other attractions of this popular resort. For those who prefer not to walk, the "Road Runner", Shanklin's road train, stops by the door (in season).
Facilities:	Room: 📶📺 General: ●✕♫ Leisure: ☂

SHANKLIN

St Leonards Hotel ◆◆◆◆ Guest Accommodation
22 Queens Road, Shanklin, PO37 6AW   SILVER AWARD

T:	+44 (0) 1983 862121
E:	info@stleonards-hotel.co.uk
W:	stleonards-hotel.co.uk
Bedrooms:	7 • sleeps 17
Prices:	Double and single: £25 per person per night breakfast included • Debit/credit card accepted
Open:	Year round except Christmas and New Year
Description:	A warm, friendly atmosphere, comfortable surroundings and freshly prepared home cooked food, combine to make your holiday just that little bit more special. Built in 1870, it is close to the famous cliff walk and the lift to Shanklin's award-winning safe, sandy beaches.
Facilities:	Room: ⬛📶📞📺🔔 General: ✂⬛✕❄

SHORWELL

Combe Barn ★★★★Self Catering
Newbarn Farm, Newbarn Lane, Newport, PO30 3JJ

T:	+44 (0) 1983 862121
W:	combebarn.co.uk
Units:	1 • sleeps 8
Prices:	From: £625-£1,500 per week
Open:	Year round except Christmas and New Year
Description:	Combe Barn is a newly converted barn on a working sheep farm in Shorwell. The local area is renowned for its stunning downland scenery and wildlife and the barn is only a 10-minute drive to Newport or the south coast beaches.
Facilities:	Room: 🛏✕ General: ⬛♨📺📶 Leisure: 🚲

TOTLAND BAY

Totland Bay YHA ★★★Hostel

Hurst Hill, Totland Bay, PO39 0HD

T:	+44 (0) 1983 752165
E:	totland@yha.org.uk
W:	yha.org.uk
Dormitories:	15 • sleeps 49
Prices:	Dormitory pricing: £9.95-£13.95 • Debit/credit card, cheques/cash accepted
Open:	Year round
Description:	Former private home and hotel, on west side of island, near cliff top walks and beaches.
Facilities:	Room: ⛄✕▥▦ General: ✕P▥✕▦▦✕▦▦▦▦

UPTON

Tithe Barn/Old Byre/The Cote ★★★★★Self Catering

Little Upton Farm, Gatehouse Road, Ryde, PO33 4BS

T:	+44 (0) 1983 563236
E:	alison@littleuptonfarm.co.uk
W:	littleuptonfarm.co.uk
Units:	3 • sleeps 16
Prices:	From £343-£864 per week
Open:	Year round
Description:	High standard barn with all en suite facilities, drying room, dishwasher, log stoves, all rooms with outstanding views over award-winning landscape. Sleeps six in the Tithe Bar and Old Byre. Sleeps 4+ in The Cote.
Facilities:	General: P▦▦▦

BRENCHLEY

Hononton Cottage ♦♦♦♦Guest Accommodation

Palmers Green Lane, Brenchley, Tonbridge, Kent, TN12 7BJ   SILVER AWARD

T:	+44 (0) 1892 722483
E:	marston.brenchley@tinyworld.co.uk
Bedrooms:	2 • sleeps 4
Prices:	Double: £65-£70 per room per night breakfast included Euros accepted
Open:	Year round except Christmas and New Year
Description:	This 16thC farmhouse is on quiet lane among apple orchards. Ideal base for walking and touring with several National Trust properties nearby.
Facilities:	Room: ⛄✕▣▥▦▦ General: ✕P▦▦▦

75

BROADSTAIRS

East Horndon Hotel ◆◆◆◆Guest Accommodation
4 Eastern Esplanade, Broadstairs, Kent, CT10 1DP   SILVER AWARD

T:	+44 (0) 1843 868306
E:	easthorndon@hotmail.com
W:	easthorndonhotel.com
Bedrooms:	9 • sleeps 16
Prices:	Double: £30-37.50; Single: £24-32; both per person per night breakfast included • Debit/credit card accepted
Open:	Year round except Christmas and New Year
Description:	Spacious rooms. Modern facilities. Fabulous views. Situated on the Eastern Esplanade (part of the scenic Viking Trail) in an unrivalled, peaceful seafront position overlooking a sandy bay and the Channel.
Facilities:	Room: ▥. General: ⅄P🕮🍷

CANTERBURY

Iffin Farmhouse ★★★★Guest Accommodation
Iffin Lane, Canterbury, Kent, CT4 7BE

T:	+44 (0) 1227 462776
E:	sarah@iffin.co.uk
W:	iffin.co.uk
Bedrooms:	3 • sleeps 7
Prices:	Double: £95.70 per room per night breakfast included
	Debit/credit card, cheques/cash accepted
Open:	Year round
Description:	A deluxe B&BG in a tucked-away rural location six minutes' drive to Canterbury centre. Recipient of a Green Tourism Award.
Facilities:	Room: ⅃✗◨🗄🖥▥📺▥🖑↻. General: ⅄P✂♨✗❋ Leisure: 🚲

CHILHAM

Castle Cottage Chilham B&B ★★★★B&B
School Hill, Chilham, Canterbury, Kent, CT4 8DE

T:	+44 (0) 1227 730330
E:	l.frankel@btinternet.com
W:	castlecottagechilham.co.uk
Bedrooms:	2 • sleeps 4
Prices:	Double: £65-£75 per room per night breakfast included Cheques/cash accepted
Open:	Year round except Christmas and New Year
Description:	Idyllic village location on Pilgrims Way. Very comfortable and welcoming cottage with secretive and magical atmosphere. Beautiful views of North Downs, garden and village square.
Facilities:	Room: 🖑▥📺↻ General: ✂❋🖼

CLIFFE WOODS

Orchard Cottage ★★★★ Guest Accommodation

11 View Road, Cliffe Woods, Rochester, ME3 8JQ   SILVER AWARD

T:	+44 (0) 1634 222780
E:	enquiries@orchardcottagekent.co.uk
W:	orchardcottagekent.co.uk
Bedrooms:	3 • sleeps 7
Prices:	Double: £50 per room per night breakfast included
Open:	Year round except Christmas and New Year
Description:	Self-contained, two-bedroomed facility with guest lounge and kitchen. A semi-rural location with guaranteed parking within gated driveway.
Facilities:	Room: 📺 General: **P**

DOVER

Westbank Guesthouse ◆◆◆◆ Guest Accommodation

239-241 Folkestone Road, Dover, Kent, CT17 9LL

T:	+44 (0) 1304 201061
E:	thewestbank@aol.com
W:	westbankguesthouse.co.uk
Bedrooms:	13 • sleeps 31
Prices:	Double: £40-£50 per room per night breakfast included; Single: £25-40 per person per night breakfast included Debit/credit card accepted cheques/cash accepted
Open:	Year round
Description:	A pleasant, Victorian building, located five minutes from docks and train and 15 minutes from Channel Tunnel. Family rooms, en suite, TV, tea-/coffee-making, off-road parking.
Facilities:	Room: 📺 General:

GRAFTY GREEN

Foxes Earth B&B ◆◆◆◆ Guest Accommodation

Headcorn Road, Grafty Green, Maidstone, Kent, ME17 2AP

T:	+44 (0) 1622 858350
E:	europa.13@btinternet.com
W:	foxesearthbedandbreakfast.co.uk
Bedrooms:	3 • sleeps 5
Prices:	Double: £45-55 per room per night breakfast included Euros accepted
Open:	Year round
Description:	Detached four-bedroom home between Lenham and Headcorn, in the heart of the Weald of Kent. Leeds Castle is 15 minutes away.
Facilities:	Room: 📺 General: **P**

HAWKHURST

4 Alma Terrace　　　　★★★★Self Catering

Booking address: Southdowns, Burwash Road, Heathfield, TN21 8TE

T:	+44 (0) 1435 868333
E:	bartonrachel@yahoo.co.uk
W:	holiday-rentals.com
Units:	1 • sleeps 4
Prices:	From £175-£300 per week
Open:	Year round
Description:	Victorian terrace with country views. Garden with patio and shed. Off-street parking. Bedrooms: one double, one twin. Near village shop and pubs. Ideal for cycling, walking and historic sites.
Facilities:	Room: ⬆✕▥TV▢▣ General: P✳▣

HOLLINGBOURNE

The Boat House　　　　★★★★Self Catering

Booking address: Pacific Delta Ltd, Lynx Business Park, Maidstone, TN17 2LR

T:	+44 (0) 1435 868333
W:	cottageonthelake.co.uk
Units:	1 • sleeps 6
Prices:	From £350-875 per week
Open:	Year round
Description:	An enchanting ragstone waterside boat house with two bedrooms, sleeping six people, set in a stunning location beside a lake/millrace. Close to Leeds Castle with many other Kent and Sussex attractions. Peaceful, rural location.
Facilities:	Room: ⬆✕▥📞TV▢▣ General: P✕▣

MAIDSTONE

The Coach House　　　　◆◆◆◆Guest Accommodation

Laddingford, Maidstone, Kent, ME18 6DB　　　　SILVER AWARD

T:	+44 (0) 1622 873390
E:	susan@thecoachhouseladdingford.co.uk
W:	thecoachhouseladdingford.co.uk
Bedrooms:	6 • sleeps 12
Prices:	Double: £55 per room per night breakfast included Debit/credit card accepted
Open:	Year round
Description:	A beautifully converted coach house dating from the 1800s set in unspoilt countryside of orchards and farmland between Laddingford and Yalding. Laddingford boasts an award-winning real-ale public house, well-marked walking routes, and cycling is also very popular.
Facilities:	Room: ⬆✕♿▥ TV General: ✕P

MEOPHAM

Feathercot Lodge ★★★★ Self Catering
New Street Road, Meopham, Gravesend, DA13 0JS

T:	+44 (0) 1474 872265
E:	feathercot@hotmail.com
W:	holidayhomeandaway.com
Units:	2 • sleeps 4
Prices:	From £300 per week
Open:	Year round
Description:	One-bedroom luxury log cabin. Fully equipped. Walk-in shower. TV, DVD, Freeview, dishwasher, microwave and washing machine. Centrally heated.
Facilities:	Room: 🖩📺🖥️🖨️ General: 🖥️

BURNLEY

Ormerod Hotel ♦♦♦ Guest Accommodation
123 Ormerod Road, Burnley, Lancashire, BB11 3QW

T:	+44 (0) 1282 423255
Bedrooms:	10 • sleeps 19
Prices:	Double: £45 per room per night breakfast included; Single: £29 per person per night breakfast included Debit/credit card accepted
Open:	Year round
Description:	The hotel has recently been refurbished to provide all rooms with en suite facilities. Opposite Queens Park, and only five minutes from the town centre.
Facilities:	Room: 🖿🖫🖩 General: 🖫🗙🖾

CHIPPING

Clark House Farm ♦♦♦♦ Guest Accommodation
Chipping, Preston, Lancashire, PR3 2GQ

T:	+44 (0) 1995 61209
E:	fpr@agriplus.net
W:	clarkhousefarm.com
Bedrooms:	2 • sleeps 4
Prices:	Double: £28 per person per night breakfast included
Open:	Year round
Description:	Situated in the heart of Lancashire's scenic Ribble Valley, the picturesque village of Chipping is located on the edge of the Forest of Bowland. Clark House Farm is 0.5 miles from the village.
Facilities:	Room: 🖫🖩📺 General: **P**

CHIPPING

Judd Holmes Barn ★★★★Self Catering

Judd Holmes Lane, Chipping, Preston, Lancashire, PR3 2TJ

T:	+44 (0) 1995 61209
W:	juddholmes.co.uk
Units:	1 • sleeps 4
Prices:	From £270-£490 per week
Open:	Year round
Description:	Beautiful 17C barn conversion adjacent to owner's farmhouse. Fully equipped, stylish decor and fantastic views.
Facilities:	Call for details

FENCE

Grains Barn Farm ★★★★★B&B
SILVER AWARD

Barrowford Road, Fence, Burnley, Lancashire, BB12 9QQ

T:	+44 (0) 1282 601320
E:	stay@grainsbarnfarm.com
W:	grainsbarnfarm.com
Bedrooms:	1 • sleeps 2
Prices:	Double: £35-£50 per room per night room only
Open:	Year round
Description:	Set within 12 acres with superb views over the surrounding countryside Grains Barn Farm is a Grade II Listed building finished to a very high standard. The en suite bedroom is downstairs with a cosy lounge upstairs among the original oak.
Facilities:	Call for details

GISBURN

Coverdale Farm ★★★★Self Catering

Howgill Lane, Gisburn, BB7 4JL

T:	+44 (0) 1200 445265
W:	coverdalefarm.co.uk
Units:	1 • sleeps 4
Prices:	From £320 per week
Open:	Year round except Christmas and New Year
Description:	Recently converted self-catering cottage which is adjoins 18thC farmhouse. Lounge, kitchen/dining room, bathroom with separate shower, one double, one twin, central heating.
Facilities:	Room: ⁑✗▥.ⓉⓋ⊟🗍🕾 General: P🐾❀◉🖵 Leisure: 🎣

LONGRIDGE

The Corporation Arms ◆◆◆◆ Guest Accommodation
Lower Road, Longridge, Preston, Lancashire, PR3 2YJ

T:	+44 (0) 1772 782644
E:	nicola@brierhey.co.uk
W:	corporationarms.co.uk
Bedrooms:	5 • sleeps 10
Prices:	Double: £52-£65per person per night breakfast included
	Debit/credit card accepted
Open:	Year round
Description:	An archetypal, traditional English country pub with beautifully restored bar and dining rooms. Five fully air conditioned bedrooms all en suite. B&B from £52. A family-run country inn with accommodation.
Facilities:	Room: ⌖✕⬛⬛🚿⬛📺📶
	General: ♨✕

PRESTON

Little Stubbins B&B ★★★★ B&B
Stubbins Lane, Claughton On Brock, Preston, Lancashire, PR3 0PL

T:	+44 (0) 1995 640376
E:	littlestubbins@aol.com
W:	littlestubbins.co.uk
Bedrooms:	3 • sleeps 6
Prices:	Double: £25 per person per night breakfast included
Open:	Year round
Description:	Little Stubbins is east of the A6 in the rural village of Claughton-on-Brock and is surrounded by peaceful farm land, between the Rivers Wyre and Brock.
Facilities:	Call for details

RIMINGTON

Raikes Barn ★★★★ Self Catering
Booking address: Beckside Farm, Cross Hill Lane, BB7 4EF

T:	+44 (0) 1200 445636
E:	elizabeth.robinson1@btinternet.com
W:	raikesbarn.co.uk
Units:	1 • sleeps 7
Prices:	From £375 per week
Open:	Year round
Description:	Formerly an 18thC stone barn, converted to a three-bedroomed house. Open coal fire in the lounge. All fuel, power, linen and towels included in rent.
Facilities:	Room: ⬛📞📺⬛⬛📶
	General: P♨🐾✕☼⬛⬛
	Leisure: 🎵

LANCASHIRE

ROSSENDALE

The Old White Horse   ♦♦♦ Guest Accommodation
211 Goodshaw Lane, Goodshaw, Rossendale, Lancashire, BB4 8DD

T:	+44 (0) 1706 215474
Bedrooms:	4 • sleeps 6
Prices:	Double: £48; Single: £26; both per person per night room only
Open:	Year round
Description:	A charmingly restored inn – now a family home – offering excellent accommodation in a quiet picturesque area with easy access to the major routes nearby.
Facilities:	Room: 🍵🛏📺📶 General: ✂🔒☂❄

SLAIDBURN

Slaidburn YHA   ★★★Hostel
Church Street, Slaidburn, Clitheroe, Lancashire, BB7 3ER

T:	+44 (0) 1282 842349
E:	slaidburn@yha.org.uk
W:	yha.org.uk
Dormitories:	Call for details
Prices:	Dormitory pricing: £10 • Debit/credit card, cheques/cash accepted
Open:	Year round
Description:	Extensively modernised former 17thC coaching inn in the centre of the village. Open fires, family rooms and meals available at the public house opposite.
Facilities:	Room: 🛏 General: ✂🔥🔒☂

THORNLEY

Loudview Barn   ★★★★Self Catering
Ramsclough Farm, Thornley, Preston, Lancashire, PR3 2TN

T:	+44 (0) 1282 842349
Units:	1 • sleeps 4
Prices:	From £220-£315 per week
Open:	Year round
Description:	Design award-winning converted barn in tranquil setting, stunning panoramic views of this unspoilt area. Furnished and equipped to the highest standards.
Facilities:	Room: 🛏📺📶 General: 🐾🔒☂❄

MOIRA

Lakeview Lodge
★★★★Self Catering

Shortheath Road, Moira, Ashby-de-la-Zouch, DE12 6BN

T:	+44 (0) 1283 763611
E:	shortheathwater@aol.com
Units:	1 • sleeps 4
Prices:	From £320-£475 per week
Open:	Year round
Description:	Lakeview Lodge offers superior self catering accommodation perfectly situated overlooking a fishing lake, creating a haven of peace and tranquillity.
Facilities:	General: P◨✿⊡ Leisure: 🚲🚶

BRACKENBOROUGH

Brackenborough Arms
★★★Hotel

Cordeux Corner, Brackenborough, Louth, Lincolnshire, LN11 0SZ

T:	+44 (0) 1507 609169
E:	info@brackenborough.co.uk
W:	brackenborough.co.uk
Bedrooms:	24 • sleeps 48
Prices:	Double: £72-£77; Single: £58.95-£64; both per room per night breakfast included • Debit/credit card, euros accepted
Open:	Year round
Description:	A purpose-built, country hotel, high standards, privately owned and personally run. On the A16 Louth to Grimsby road, two miles from Louth with an outstanding name for food.
Facilities:	Room: ✕⬜⬆🔥📺🖥 General: ◐◨⬛✂🚗✕✿ Leisure: 🚶

COLSTERWORTH

York House
★★★★B&B

Bourne Road, Grantham, Lincolnshire, NG33 5JE

T:	+44 (0) 1476 861955
E:	rkyorkhouse@dsl.pipex.com
Bedrooms:	1 • sleeps 2
Prices:	Double: £60-£70 per room per night breakfast included
Open:	Year round
Description:	York House is situated in the village of Colsterworth, 0.25 miles from the A1 on the B676.
Facilities:	Room: ⬜ General: P✿🔥

COLSTERWORTH

Byards Leap Cottage ★★★B&B

Byards Leap, Cranwell, Sleaford, Lincolnshire, NG34 8EY

T:	+44 (0) 1400 261537
Bedrooms:	2 • sleeps 4
Prices:	Double: £20 per person per night breakfast included
Open:	Year round
Description:	A country cottage of local Ancaster stone, surrounded by attractive gardens and on the Viking Way long distance footpath.
Facilities:	Room: 🕯✕🗄🛢🅰📺🔔 General: ⚡✕☀🄿

DIGBY

Woodend Farm B&B ◆◆◆Guest Accommodation

Woodend Farm, Digby, Lincoln, Lincolnshire, LN4 3NG

T:	+44 (0) 1526 860347
Bedrooms:	3 • sleeps 7
Prices:	Double: £18-£20 per person per night breakfast included Cheques/cash accepted
Open:	Year round
Description:	A homely farmhouse overlooking paddock and wood. Access all day. Guests' own sitting room with log fire. Good food at local pub. Central for Lincoln, Grantham and Boston. Convenient for RAF Cranwell and Digby.
Facilities:	Room: 🗄🛢🅰📺🔔🔥 General: 🖼⚡✕☀🄿 Leisure: ∪🐎⏵

GEDNEY HILL

The Dukes Head Inn ◆◆◆Guest Accommodation

49 Highstock Lane, Gedney Hill, Spalding, Lincolnshire, PE12 0QQ

T:	+44 (0) 1406 330275
Bedrooms:	3 • sleeps 6
Prices:	Double and single: £24.99 per person per night breakfast included • Debit/credit card accepted
Open:	Year round
Description:	Old country inn with one bar, facilities for pub games and modern block at rear with B&B.
Facilities:	Room: 🕯✕🅰📺 General: 🅿🖼⚡✕☀🄿 Leisure: 🐎⏵

LINCOLN

Good Lane B&B ★★★B&B

31 Good Lane, Lincoln, Lincolnshire, LN1 3EH

T:	+44 (0) 1522 542994
E:	sue@goodlane.co.uk
W:	goodlane.co.uk
Bedrooms:	3 • sleeps 5
Prices:	Double and single: £25 per person per night breakfast included • Euros accepted
Open:	Year round except Christmas and New Year
Description:	Home from home. Georgian house. Quiet street. Within a few minutes' walk of the cathedral, old town, shops and restaurants.
Facilities:	Room: (symbols) General: (symbols) Leisure: (symbol)

MARKET RASEN

Beechwood Guesthouse ◆◆◆◆Guest Accommodation

54 Willingham Road, Market Rasen, Lincolnshire, LN8 3DX

T:	+44 (0) 1673 844043
E:	beechwoodgh@aol.com
W:	beechwoodguesthouse.co.uk
Bedrooms:	1 • sleeps 2
Prices:	Double: £49 room only
Open:	Year round
Description:	Beechwood guesthouse is a period property set back from the road in a third of an acre of landscaped gardens. The bedrooms are individually decorated to a high standard, with usual amenities. One bedroom is on ground floor.
Facilities:	Room: (symbols) General: (symbols)

SOUTH HYKEHAM

Welbeck Cottage ★★★★B&B

19 Meadow Lane, South Hykeham, Lincoln, Lincolnshire, LN6 9PF

T:	+44 (0) 1522 692669
E:	mad@wellbeck1.demon.co.uk
Bedrooms:	3 • sleeps 6
Prices:	Double: £40 per room per night breakfast included Cheques/cash accepted
Open:	Year round
Description:	Two double, one twin en suite rooms in quiet rural location. Friendly, personal service.
Facilities:	Room: (symbols) General: (symbols)

SWAYFIELD

Woodview   ★★★Self Catering
Booking address: Lucklaw House, 13 Corby Road, Swayfield, Grantham, NG33 4LQ

T:	+44 (0) 1476 550097
E:	bears178@aol.com
Units:	1 • sleeps 4
Prices:	From £150-£280 per week • Cheques/cash accepted
Open:	Year round
Description:	Self-contained well appointed 1st floor apartment in a quiet rural village. Close to Stamford, Burghley House and Rutland Water.
Facilities:	General: P✂❀▤ Leisure: ▶

TETFORD

Poachers Hideaway   Self Catering rating applied for
Flintwood Farm, Belchford, Horncastle, Lincolnshire, LN9 6QN

T:	+44 (0) 1507 533555
E:	andrewtuxworth@poachershideaway.com
Units:	6 • sleeps 26
Prices:	From £100-£559 per week • Debit/credit card accepted
Open:	Year round except Christmas and New Year
Description:	Explore our 170 acres of private woodland, wild flower pasture, natural hedgerows and water meadows, fishing in our lakes.
Facilities:	General: P✂❀▤ Leisure: U🚲♪▶

BESTHORPE

The Hayloft and The Granary   ★★★Self Catering
Mayfield Barn, Silver Street, Besthorpe, NR17 2LE

T:	+44 (0) 1953 455589
E:	mayfieldaccommodation@fsmail.net
W:	mayfieldbarn.co.uk
Units:	2 • sleeps 12
Prices:	From £310-£410 per week
Open:	Year round
Description:	Sympathetically converted barn, standing in five acres. Comfortable, well thought out accommodation to suit a range of ages.
Facilities:	General: ❀

NORFOLK

BIRCHAM

The Kings Head Hotel ♦♦♦Guest Accommodation
Lynn Road, Bircham, King's Lynn, Norfolk, PE31 6RJ   SILVER AWARD

T:	+44 (0) 1485 578266
E:	welcome@the-kings-head-bircham.co.uk
W:	the-kings-head-bircham.co.uk
Bedrooms:	9 • sleeps 18
Prices:	Double: £69.50 per room per night breakfast included
Open:	Year round except Christmas and New Year
Description:	This beautiful, Grade II Listed building has been refurbished to create one of the most contemporary hotels and restaurants in Norfolk.
Facilities:	Call for details

BRANTHILL

Canary Cottage ★★★Self Catering
Branthill Farm, Wells-next-the-Sea, Norfolk, NR23 1SB

T:	+44 (0) 1328 710246
E:	branthill.farms@macunlimited.net
W:	therealaleshop.co.uk
Units:	1 • sleeps 2
Prices:	From £217 per week
Open:	Year round
Description:	Charmingly situated, well-equipped single-storey cottage, close to meadows and historic farm buildings. Ideal for experiencing coast and countryside.
Facilities:	General: ✿ Leisure: ℺

COLBY

Bay Cottage ★★★★Self Catering
Colby Corner, Colby, Aylsham, Norfolk, NR11 7EB

T:	+44 (0) 1263 734574
E:	jsclarke@colbycorner.fsnet.co.uk
W:	enchantingcottages.co.uk
Units:	2 • sleeps 7
Prices:	From £294 per week
Open:	Year round
Description:	This delightful, well-furnished property, once a pair of farm workers' cottages, has been converted to three-bedroomed accommodation. Set in a lovely half acre garden of fruit trees and lawns.
Facilities:	General: ✿ Leisure: ⬠

HUNSTANTON

The Gables ★★★★Guest Accommodation

Austin Street, Hunstanton, Norfolk, PE36 6AW

T:	+44 (0) 1485 532514
Bedrooms:	5 • sleeps 13
Prices:	Double: £22-£28 per person per night breakfast included Debit/credit card, cheques/cash accepted
Open:	Year round
Description:	A large, Edwardian house, newly renovated near to seafront. All rooms en suite. A warm and friendly welcome awaits.
Facilities:	Room: ✗▣🔥🎤📺🖥📻 General: ✗🛇⌕✕❄🔥

LITTLE SNORING

Jex Farm Barns ★★★★Self Catering

Jex Farm Barn, Little Snoring, NR21 0JJ

T:	+44 (0) 1328 878257
E:	stephenharvey@supanet.com
W:	broadland.com/jexfarmbarn.html
Units:	1 • sleeps 5
Prices:	From £560 per week
Open:	Year round
Description:	Converted in 2003/4 from a derelict cart shed with exposed beams and wooden floors using reclaimed materials. On a small family farm surrounded by meadows with a small wood to the rear. A fully-enclosed garden with patio, garden furniture and BBQ, parking for three cars.
Facilities:	General: P❄

OVERSTRAND

Green Lawn House ★★★Self Catering

35 High Street, Overstrand, Norfolk, NR27 0AB

T:	+44 (0) 1263 576925
E:	inquiries@greenlawnhouse.co.uk
W:	greenlawnhouse.co.uk
Units:	3 • sleeps 8
Prices:	From £195-425 per week
Open:	Year round
Description:	Green Lawn House is located within the quaint fishing village of Overstrand offering a choice of three splendid apartments, four minutes to the sea.
Facilities:	Call for details

WEST RAYNHAM

Pollywiggle Cottage ★★★★Self Catering

Booking address: 79 Earlham Road, Norwich, NR2 3RE

T:	+44 (0) 1603 471990
E:	marilyn@pollywigglecottage.co.uk
Units:	1 • sleeps 8
Prices:	From £340-£800 per week • Cheques/cash accepted
Open:	Year round
Description:	A pretty brick and flintstone semi-detached cottage lying in the heart of the rural North Norfolk countryside. Sea is 15 miles away.
Facilities:	General: P✘❄▢

WORSTEAD

Woodcarvers Barn ★★★★Self Catering

Rose Cottage, Honing Row, Worstead, Norfolk, NR28 9RH

T:	+44 (0) 1692 536662
E:	si@worstead.co.uk
W:	worstead.co.uk/barn
Units:	1 • sleeps 5
Prices:	From £250-£475 per week
Open:	Year round
Description:	Just completed and furnished to a high standard. Two-bedroomed barn conversion in historic wool village of Worstead in North Norfolk.
Facilities:	General: ❄

ARTHINGWORTH

The Bull's Head ★★★Inn

Kelmarsh Road, Market Harborough, Northamptonshire, LE16 8JZ

T:	+44 (0) 1858 525637
E:	thebullshead@btconnect.com
W:	thebullsheadonline.co.uk
Bedrooms:	8 • sleeps 21
Prices:	Double: £55-£65; Single: £40-£45; both per room per night breakfast included • Debit/credit card accepted
Open:	Year round
Description:	The Bull's Head is an independent, family-run business and we pride ourselves on doing all we can to make our customers feel welcome and comfortable. We are ideally situated in the peaceful Northamptonshire countryside.
Facilities:	Room: ⅍✘TV▢☏ General: P♠♦🚗✕❄

BRAUNSTON

The Old Workshop ★★★★B&B

The Old Workshop, The Wharf, Daventry, Northamptonshire, NN11 7JQ

T:	+44 (0) 1788 891421
E:	info@the-old-workshop.com
W:	the-old-work`shop.com
Bedrooms:	2 • sleeps 4
Prices:	Double: £55 per room per night breakfast included
Open:	Year round
Description:	Delightful canal-side B&B. Walking distance from pubs. Quality en suite bedrooms (TV, DVD, video, tea/coffee). Farm produce breakfast. Off road parking and garden.
Facilities:	Room: ⛛🛏🖵📺🖵 General: ✂�ᴘ🕮❈🛱

WOODNEWTON

Bridge Cottage ★★★★B&B

Oundle Road, Peterborough, Northamptonshire, PE8 5EG

T:	+44 (0) 1780 470779
E:	enquiries@bridgecottage.net
W:	bridgecottage.net
Bedrooms:	3 • sleeps 6
Prices:	Double: £50-£75 per person per night room only
Open:	Year round except Christmas
Description:	Bridge Cottage is a recently renovated property situated on the edge of the village of Woodnewton within walking distance of the local pub. We have superb views over open countryside with a river running at the bottom of the garden.
Facilities:	Room: 🖵⛛🛏🖵 General: ᴘ❈🛱

ALNHAM

The Lodge and the Gatehouse ★★★★Self Catering

Alnham, Alnwick, Northumberland, NE66 4TJ

T:	+44 (0) 1669 630210
E:	jenny@alnhamfarm.co.uk
W:	alnhamfarm.co.uk
Units:	2 • sleeps 10
Prices:	From £200-£460 per week • Euros accepted
Open:	Year round
Description:	These comfortable cottages with enclosed garden, offer an excellent peaceful base to explore Northumberland. Tennis court and fishing available. Pets welcome.
Facilities:	Room: 🖵 General: ᴘ🕮✂ᴊ❈🛥🖵 Leisure: ⚲ᴊ

ALNMOUTH

Seafield House B&B ◆◆◆ Guest Accommodation

18 Northumberland Street, Alnmouth, Alnwick, Northumberland, NE66 2RJ

T:	+44 (0) 1665 833256
E:	jilly@seafieldhouse.co.uk
W:	seafieldhouse.co.uk
Bedrooms:	6 • sleeps 10
Prices:	Double: £30-£40; Single: £35-£40; both per person per night breakfast included
Open:	Year round except Christmas and New Year
Description:	Seafield House offers luxury en suite bedrooms and a hearty breakfast in central Alnmouth village – an ever-popular Northumberland coastal location.
Facilities:	Room: 🖳🗲📺📶 General: ✂🛎♨⚙☼🅿 Leisure: ♪🏃

ALNWICK

Herring Sheds Cottage ★★★★★ Self Catering

Booking address: Henhill and Birchwood Hall Cottages,
Alnwick Castle, Belford, NE70 7JQ

T:	+44 (0) 1668 219941
E:	jane@nehc.co.uk
W:	alnwickcastlecottages.co.uk
Units:	1 • sleeps 4
Prices:	From £305-£620 per week • Debit/credit card, euros accepted
Open:	Year round except Christmas and New Year
Description:	A superbly equipped and well positioned cottage for four opening onto the beach of a tiny fishing village. Open all year.
Facilities:	Room: 🛏 General: P✂♨☼📺📶

ALNWICK

Prudhoe Croft ★★★★ B&B

11 Prudhoe Street, Alnwick, Northumberland, NE66 1UW   SILVER AWARD

T:	+44 (0) 1665 606197
E:	prudhoecroft@supanet.com
W:	prudhoecroft.co.uk
Bedrooms:	2 • sleeps 2
Prices:	Double: £30-£32.50 per person per night breakfast included Cheques/cash accepted
Open:	Year round except Christmas and New Year
Description:	Victorian townhouse in centre of Alnwick, within few minutes' walk of Alnwick Castle and Garden. South facing enclosed garden.
Facilities:	Room: 🖳🗲📺📶 General: P♨☼☀🅿

ALNWICK

Rock Midstead Organic Farm House ★★★ Farmhouse

Rock, Alnwick, Northumberland, NE66 2TH

T:	+44 (0) 1665 579225
E:	ian@rockmidstead.co.uk
W:	rockmidstead.co.uk
Bedrooms:	3 • sleeps 7
Prices:	Double: £30 per person per night breakfast included Debit/credit card accepted
Open:	Year round except Christmas and New Year
Description:	Peaceful farmhouse on working farm with excellent views of the countryside. Freshly-baked bread daily. Lovely afternoon teas in the farm shop.
Facilities:	Room: ⌨✕⊑✦▥ⓉⓋ🥄 General: ✂Ⓟ▥♣✕ Leisure: ▶

ALNWICK

Roseworth ★★★★B&B

Alnmouth Road, Alnwick, Northumberland, NE66 2PR

T:	+44 (0) 1665 603911
E:	roseworth@tiscali.co.uk
W:	roseworthalnwick.co.uk
Bedrooms:	3 • sleeps 6
Prices:	Double: £27-£30 per person per night breakfast included Cheques/cash accepted
Open:	Year round except Christmas and New Year
Description:	Semi-detached, private home set in large gardens. Ample parking in quiet residential area to the south of Alnwick on Alnmouth Road. Non-smoking establishment.
Facilities:	Room: ⌨✕⊑✦▥ⓉⓋ🥄✎ General: ✂✕☀♨ Leisure: 🚲

ALNWICK

The Old Smithy ★★★★Self Catering

Booking address: 1 West Turn Pike, Glanton, NE66 4AN

T:	07970 210607
E:	k.keers@tiscali.co.uk
Units:	1 • sleeps 6
Prices:	From £295-£695 per week • Euros accepted
Open:	Year round
Description:	The cottage, formerly a blacksmiths, provides a high standard of comfortable accommodation in the heart of this delightful Northumberland village.
Facilities:	Room: ▥ General: ▥✕🔌☀▣▯

ALWINTON

Fellside Cottage
★★★★Self Catering

Bedlington Lane Farm, Bedlington, NE22 6AA

T:	+44 (0) 1670 823042
E:	stay@fellsidecottcheviots.co.uk
W:	fellsidecottcheviots.co.uk
Units:	1 • sleeps 3
Prices:	From £195-£495 per week
Open:	Year round except Christmas and New Year
Description:	Cosy cottage nestling in peaceful hamlet within National Park. Well equipped, open fire, lovely garden. Wonderful views. Country pub opposite.
Facilities:	General: P🏠♨☆📶

AMBLE

Harbour Guesthouse
★★★Guesthouse

24 Lezers Street, Amble, Morpeth, Northumberland, NE65 0AA

T:	+44 (0) 1665 710381
Bedrooms:	6 • sleeps 11
Prices:	Double and single: £27.50 per person per night breakfast included • Debit/credit card accepted
Open:	Year round except Christmas and New Year
Description:	The Harbour Guesthouse and restaurant has six letting rooms all en suite. Situated on Amble Harbour, three minutes to town centre.
Facilities:	Room: ⬛✖♨🏠📺📶 General: ✄P🏠♨☆📶✖☆🔌

BARDON MILL

Gibbs Hill Farm
♦♦♦♦Guest Accommodation

Once Brewed, Hexham, Northumberland, NE47 7AP

T:	+44 (0) 1434 344030
E:	val@gibbshillfarm.co.uk
W:	gibbshillfarm.co.uk
Bedrooms:	3 • sleeps 6
Prices:	Double: £28-£30 per person per night breakfast included Debit/credit card, cheques/cash accepted
Open:	Year round except Christmas and New Year
Description:	A 750-acre working, family farm on Hadrian's Wall. Large, comfortable rooms with breathtaking views. Ideal for walking, peaceful by pretty lake.
Facilities:	Room: ⬛✖♨🏠📺🔌 General: ✄🏠♨☆✖☆🔌 Leisure: ∪♪▶

BARDON MILL

Maple Lodge B&B ★★★★B&B

Birkshaw, Hexham, Northumberland, NE47 7JL

T:	+44 (0) 1434 344365
E:	tonyarmstrong@tiscali.co.uk
W:	maplelodge-hadrianswall.co.uk
Bedrooms:	3 • sleeps 8
Prices:	Double: £28.50 per person per night breakfast included
Open:	Year round except Christmas
Description:	Maple Lodge is a 16thC Bastle House next to Vindolanda. An ideal base to visit Hadrian's Wall and Northumberland's many attractions.
Facilities:	Room: ⁸✕ᗡᕮ♨🎮📺⊡🖉 General: ⅍P⍩✿ Leisure: ∪♺⊩

BERWICK-UPON-TWEED

Cara House ♦♦♦Guest Accommodation

44 Castlegate, Berwick-Upon-Tweed, Northumberland, TD15 1JT

T:	+44 (0) 1289 302749
E:	pam@carahouse.co.uk
W:	carahouse.co.uk
Bedrooms:	2 • sleeps 6
Prices:	Double: £25-£35per person per night breakfast included Euros accepted
Open:	Year round
Description:	Centrally located two minutes' walk from town centre and railway station. Spacious rooms, off-road private parking with secure cycle storage.
Facilities:	Room: ⁸✕ᗡᕮ♨🎮📺🖉⚁ General: ⅍P⍩ Leisure: ♺♩

BERWICK-UPON-TWEED

Cobbled Yard Hotel ♦♦♦Guest Accommodation

40 Walkergate, Berwick-Upon-Tweed, Northumberland, TD15 1DJ

T:	+44 (0) 1289 308407
E:	cobbledyardhotel@berwick35.fsnet.co.uk
W:	cobbledyardhotel.com
Bedrooms:	6 • sleeps 15
Prices:	Double: £35; Single: £40-45; both per person per night breakfast included • Debit/credit card, euros accepted
Open:	Year round
Description:	This establishment was built in 1913 and has some interesting architectural features.
Facilities:	Room: ᗡᕮ♨🎮📺🖉 General: P🏧🍴⍩⭐✕ Leisure: ♩⊩

BERWICK-UPON-TWEED

Newt Cottage ★★★★ Self Catering

Hunting Hall Farm, Berwick-upon-Tweed, Northumberland, TD15 2TP

T:	+44 (0) 1289 388652
E:	kburn.huntinghall@btinternet.com
Units:	1 • sleeps 4
Prices:	From £293-£470 per week
Open:	Year round
Description:	This unique farm cottage with traditional Tweed range has been lovingly restored to offer an environmentally-friendly holiday in tranquil surroundings.
Facilities:	Room: ▥ General: ⚓☼▱

BERWICK-UPON-TWEED

West Coates ◆◆◆◆◆ Guest Accommodation

30 Castle Terrace, Berwick-Upon-Tweed,
Northumberland, TD15 1NZ

GOLD AWARD

T:	+44 (0) 1289 309666
E:	karenbrownwestcoates@yahoo.com
W:	westcoates.co.uk
Bedrooms:	3 • sleeps 6
Prices:	Double: £45-£50 per person per night breakfast included Debit/credit card, euros accepted
Open:	Year round
Description:	West Coates, comfortable Georgian townhouse set in two acres of gardens. Excellent home cooking. Facilities include indoor pool and hot tub.
Facilities:	Room: ♨✕⛁♨▥⊡☜ General: ⊬P⚒✕☼♨ Leisure: ∪♨♪⚘

BINGFIELD

The Hytte ★★★★★ Self Catering

Bingfield, Hexham, Northumberland, NE46 4HR

T:	+44 (0) 1434 672321
E:	sgregory001@tiscali.co.uk
W:	thehytte.com
Units:	1 • sleeps 8
Prices:	From £440-£850 per week • Debit/credit card, euros accepted
Open:	Year round except Christmas and New Year
Description:	Norwegian-style mountain lodge with grass roof, situated in open countryside near Hadrian's Wall. Private garden, sauna and hot-tub.
Facilities:	Room: ▥ General: P⛁⚒♨☼⊡▱ Leisure: ∪♪

CATTON

Station House Flat ★★★ Self Catering

Station House, Catton, Hexham, NE47 9QF

T:	+44 (0) 1434 683362
E:	info@allendale-holidays.co.uk
W:	allendale-holidays.co.uk
Units:	1 • sleeps 6
Prices:	From £175-£350 per week
Open:	Year round except Christmas and New Year
Description:	A mile by riverside walk from attractive Allendale and part of railway station on a long-closed line. Walks abound.
Facilities:	Room: 🛏️ General: P🐕🅰️📷 Leisure: ♪🏃

CHATHILL

Henhill/Birchwood Hall Cottages ★★★★ Self Catering

Henhill and Birchwood Hall Cottages, Seahouses, Alnwick, NE70 7JQ

T:	+44 (0) 1668 219941
E:	jane@nehc.co.uk
W:	alnwickcastlecottages.co.uk
Units:	5 • sleeps 21
Prices:	From £280-£690 per week • Debit/credit card, euros accepted
Open:	Year round except Christmas and New Year
Description:	Stone cottages in peaceful countryside with spacious, comfortable living accommodation, log fires and well-equipped kitchens. Near beaches, castles and hills. Ideal for exploring Northumberland. No stairs.
Facilities:	General: P🅰️🍴🐕☼📷🔲 Leisure: ∪♪

CHATTON

Percy Arms Hotel ♦♦♦♦ Guest Accommodation

Main Road, Alnwick, Northumberland, NE66 5PS

T:	+44 (0) 1668 215244
E:	dfsmunro@btinternet.com
W:	percyarmshotel.co.uk
Bedrooms:	8 • sleeps 15
Prices:	Double and single: £35 per person per night breakfast included Debit/credit card, cheques/cash accepted
Open:	Year round except Christmas and New Year
Description:	Ideally situated in the heart of rural Northumberland, the Percy Arms provides a welcoming atmosphere to eat, drink and stay.
Facilities:	Room: ♨️✗📺♿🛁📺🛏️ General: P🅿️🍴🐕☼🚌✗☼🅿️ Leisure: ∪♪🏇🏃

CORBRIDGE

April Cottage
★★★★ Self Catering

Booking address: 21 Woodland Close, Chelford, Macclesfield, SK11 9BZ

T:	+44 (0) 1625 861718
E:	peterandkatedean@btopenworld.com
W:	aprilcottagecorbridge.co.uk
Units:	1 • sleeps 5
Prices:	From £300-£400 per week
Open:	Year round
Description:	A 19thC stone cottage. Accommodation comprises living-room, kitchen/dining-room, two bedrooms, one with washbasin, bathroom shower and bidet and sheltered garden.
Facilities:	General: ✖❀⊟

CRASTER

13 Rock Ville
★★★★ Self Catering

Booking address: c/o Rock Ville, 19 Heugh Road, Alnwick, NE66 3TJ

T:	+44 (0) 1665 576286
E:	rockville@barkpots.co.uk
W:	rockvillecraster.co.uk
Units:	1 • sleeps 7
Prices:	From £199-£675 per week • Debit/credit card, euros accepted
Open:	Year round except Christmas and New Year
Description:	Luxury holiday home overlooking the sea with garden leading onto rocks. Midweek and weekend breaks available low season.
Facilities:	Room: ▦ General: P❦✖❀❖⊟⊟ Leisure: ∪►

CRASTER

Craster Pine Lodges
★★★★ Self Catering

Booking address: 19 Heugh Road, Alnwick, NE66 3TJ

T:	+44 (0) 1665 576286
E:	rockville@barkpots.co.uk
W:	crasterpinelodges.co.uk
Units:	2 • sleeps 10
Prices:	From £199-£595 per week • Debit/credit card, euros accepted
Open:	Year round
Description:	Near Craster harbour. One lodge suitable for disabled. Private site. Garden, parking, pets welcome.
Facilities:	General: P✖❀★► ⊟ Leisure: ∪►

FEATHERSTONE

The Wallace Arms ★★★★Inn

Featherstone, Haltwhistle, Northumberland, NE49 0JF

T:	+44 (0) 1434 321872
E:	thewallacearms@aol.com
Bedrooms:	2 • sleeps 4
Prices:	Double: £30 per person per night breakfast included Debit/credit card, euros accepted
Open:	Year round
Description:	Character inn, rebuilt in 1850 of local stone, situated on Northern edge of Pennines, four miles from Hadrian's Wall.
Facilities:	Room: ↕✕⊡🕯🛏💻📺🕭 General: P🛈🛗♨🛎✕❄🛡 Leisure: ♪🏃

FENWICK

The Manor House ★★★★B&B

7 The Village, Berwick-Upon-Tweed, Northumberland, TD15 2PQ

T:	+44 (0) 1289 381016
E:	katemoore@homecall.co.uk
W:	manorhousefenwick.co.uk
Bedrooms:	3 • sleeps 8
Prices:	Double: £25-£35 per person per night breakfast included Euros accepted
Open:	Year round except Christmas and New Year
Description:	Situated in the small hamlet of Fenwick, only five minutes from Holy Island. The Manor House offers quality B&B in en suite rooms.
Facilities:	Room: ↕✕⊡🕯🛏💻📺🕭 General: ⊬P🛈♨✕🚍❄🛡 Leisure: ♾♪🏃

FOURSTONES

Rosebank Cottage ★★★Self Catering

Booking address: c/o Rosebank Cottage, 9a Elsinore Road, London, SE23 2SH

T:	07816 909737
E:	info@rosebankcottage.co.uk
W:	rosebankcottage.co.uk
Units:	1 • sleeps up to 4
Prices:	From £125-£250 per week • Euros accepted
Open:	Year round except Christmas and New Year
Description:	High quality accommodation, traditional stone cottage with breathtaking views of South Tyne Valley. Ideal for walkers, sleeps two-four.
Facilities:	General: P✕❄🖥 Leisure: 🚲

GREENHEAD

YHA Greenhead
★★★Hostel

Station Road, Greenhead, Brampton, Northumberland, CA8 7HG

T:	+44 (0) 1697 747401
E:	greenhead@yha.org.uk
W:	yha.org.uk
Dormitories:	6 • sleeps 40
Prices:	Dormitory pricing: £9-£16 • Debit/credit card accepted
Open:	Year round except Christmas and New Year
Description:	A converted Methodist Chapel ideally situated for walking or cycling along Hadrian's Wall and the Pennine Way.
Facilities:	Room: ⬛✖️▥📺 General: ✖️🚫♨️🚐✖️🔧♨️▣ Leisure: ♦

HALTWHISTLE

Wydon Farm B&B
★★★★Farmhouse

Wydon Farm, Haltwhistle, Northumberland, NE49 0LG

T:	+44 (0) 1434 321702
E:	stay@wydon-haltwhistle.co.uk
W:	wydon-haltwhistle.co.uk
Bedrooms:	3 • sleeps 8
Prices:	Double: £32-£36 per person per night breakfast included Debit/credit card accepted
Open:	Year round
Description:	Working farm owned by the National Trust. Easy access to Hadrian's Wall, Sustrans, cycleway and various footpaths.
Facilities:	Room: ⬛✖️📧♨️▥📺🔧 General: ✖️P🚫♨️ Leisure: 🚴🔧▶

HARBOTTLE

The Byre Vegetarian B&B
★★★★B&B
SILVER AWARD

Harbottle, Morpeth, Northumberland, NE65 7DG

T:	+44 (0) 1669 650476
E:	rosemary@the-byre.co.uk
W:	the-byre.co.uk
Bedrooms:	2 • sleeps 4
Prices:	Double: £28-£35 per person per night breakfast included Euros accepted
Open:	Year round except Christmas and New Year
Description:	Beautiful, stone-built farm byre conversion in the historic village of Harbottle. Non-smoking, vegetarian B&B. Home-cooked evening meal and packed lunches by arrangement.
Facilities:	Room: ⬛✖️▥📺🔧 General: ✖️P🚫✖️♨️▣

HAYDON BRIDGE

Grindon Cart Shed ★★★★B&B

Haydon Bridge, Hexham, Northumberland, NE47 6NQ

T:	+44 (0) 1434 684273
E:	cart shed@grindon.force9.co.uk
W:	grindon-cart shed.co.uk
Bedrooms:	3 • sleeps 6
Prices:	Double: £30 per person per night breakfast included
Open:	Year round except Christmas and New Year
Description:	A warm welcome awaits at the beautifully converted cart shed within walking distance of Hadrian's Wall. Ideal location for touring.
Facilities:	Room: ♨✕⛶🔥🛏.📺📶 General: ⚟P✗✕☼🅿

HEDDON-ON-THE-WALL

Houghton North Farm ★★★★Hostel

Heddon On The Wall, Newcastle Upon Tyne, Northumberland, NE15 0EZ

T:	+44 (0) 1661 854364
E:	wjlaws@btconnect.com
W:	hadrianswallaccommodation.com
Dormitories:	6 • sleeps 22
Prices:	Dormitory pricing: £22-£30 • Debit/credit card accepted
Open:	Year round except Christmas and New Year
Description:	Private hostel comprising six bunk-bed rooms, two en suite, with fitted kitchen, lounge and drying facilities. Adjacent to Hadrian's Wall.
Facilities:	Room: ♨✕🛏. General: P✗☼🅿🗖

HOWICK

The Old Rectory ★★★★B&B

Howick, Alnwick, Northumberland, NE66 3LE

T:	+44 (0) 1665 577590
E:	david@bbi-ltd.co.uk
W:	oldrectoryhowick.co.uk
Bedrooms:	3 • sleeps 6
Prices:	Double: £30-£35 per person per night breakfast included
Open:	Year round
Description:	Luxury country house B&B accommodation near Craster, Alnwick, Northumberland on the Heritage Coast
Facilities:	Room: ♨✕⛶🔥🛏.📺📶 General: P🅿✗✕☼🅿 Leisure: ⚲♪▸

HUMSHAUGH

Greencarts Farm   ♦♦♦ Guest Accommodation

Humshaugh, Hexham, Northumberland, NE46 4BW

T:	+44 (0) 1434 681320
E:	sandra@greencarts.co.uk
W:	greencarts.co.uk
Bedrooms:	3 • sleeps 6
Prices:	Double: £25-£40 per person per night breakfast included Euros accepted
Open:	Year round
Description:	Working farm in Roman Wall country, magnificent views. Log fires, comfortable and friendly atmosphere, ideal for exploring the area. Especially good for walkers.
Facilities:	Room: ✴✕⬜☐📶▥📺☜ General: ✕P♨☒✕❄ Leisure: ∪♪

LANGLEY-ON-TYNE

The Waiting Room   ★★★★ Self Catering

Staward Station, Hexham, Northumberland, NE47 5NR

T:	+44 (0) 1434 683030
E:	info@debhumble.co.uk
Units:	1 • sleeps 2
Prices:	From £200-£495 per week • Euros accepted
Open:	Year round
Description:	1850s detached south-facing cottage, gardens, refurbished to very high standard many original features, uninterrupted views, much wildlife, squirrels, birds and deer.
Facilities:	General: P☒❄📠☜ Leisure: ∪♨♪

LONGHOUGHTON

Chestnut Tree House   ♦♦♦ Guest Accommodation

7 Crowlea Road, Alnwick, Northumberland, NE66 3AN

T:	+44 (0) 1665 577153
E:	janetholtuk@btinternet.com
Bedrooms:	2 • sleeps 4
Prices:	Double: £30-£40 per person per night breakfast included Euros accepted
Open:	Year round
Description:	Chestnut Tree House, comfortable B&B accommodation, twin or double en suite bedrooms, rural location, close to the sea.
Facilities:	Room: ✴✕⬜☐📶▥📺☐☜ General: ✕P♨☒ Leisure: ♪⬆

LUCKER

Lucker Hall Steading — Self Catering rating applied for

Booking address: Alnwick Castle, Northumberland, NE70 7JQ

T:	+44 (0) 1668 219941
E:	jane@nehc.co.uk
W:	alnwickcastlecottages.co.uk
Units:	6 • sleeps 22
Prices:	From £290-£830 per week • Debit/credit card, euros accepted
Open:	Year round
Description:	A small group of superbly renovated cottages offering peace and excellent facilities at the heart of a tiny village close to Bamburgh. With beaches, castles and National Park to explore.
Facilities:	Room: ▥ General: P▥Y☓ả✿◉▯ Leisure: ♪

LUCKER

Lucker Mill — ★★★★★ Self Catering

Lucker Mill, Lucker, Belford, Northumberland, NE70 7JQ

T:	+44 (0) 1668 219941
E:	jane@nehc.co.uk
W:	alnwickcastlecottages.co.uk
Units:	2 • sleeps 12
Prices:	From £315-£820 per week • Debit/credit card, euros accepted
Open:	Year round except Christmas and New Year
Description:	Superb, newly-converted mill offering the best in comfort, facilities include en suite rooms and four-poster beds. In tiny village near Bamburgh. Sleeps five-six or 12 guests.
Facilities:	Room: ▥✍ General: P▥Y☓ả✿◉▯ Leisure: ♪

MATFEN

Matfen High House — ♦♦♦♦ Guest Accommodation

Matfen, Newcastle Upon Tyne, Northumberland, NE20 0RG

T:	+44 (0) 1661 886592
E:	struan@struan.enterprise-plc.com
Bedrooms:	4 • sleeps 8
Prices:	Double: £20-£35 per person per night breakfast included
Open:	Year round
Description:	Spacious stone-built former farmhouse, dating from 1735, in quiet rural location one mile north of Hadrian's Wall and Trail.
Facilities:	Room: ▥✕◨✦▥.ﺍ⊤⅁▥◰ General: ⅂P▲☓ả✿ Leisure: ▶

MELDON PARK

Meldon Park ★★★Self Catering

Meldon Park, Morpeth, Northumberland, NE61 3SW

T:	+44 (0) 1670 772622
E:	mrscookson@compuserve.com
W:	cottageguide.co.uk/meldonpark
Units:	1 • sleeps 4
Prices:	From £300-£400 per week • Cheques/cash accepted
Open:	Year round except Christmas and New Year
Description:	Meldon Park was designed and built in 1832 by Dobson. Meldon has a strong atmosphere of solidarity, restrained wealth and harmony in a Greek revival style.
Facilities:	Room: 🖳 General: P🗙🅰♨🖥 Leisure: ∪♪

MOHOPE

YHA Ninebanks ★★★Hostel

Orchard House, Mohope, Hexham, Northumberland, NE47 8DQ

T:	+44 (0) 1434 345288
E:	ninebanks@yha.org.uk
W:	yha.ninebanks.org.uk
Dormitories:	7 • sleeps 36
Prices:	Dormitory pricing: £8.95-£11.95 • Debit/credit card accepted
Open:	Year round except Christmas and New Year
Description:	A 250-year-old lead miner's cottage on the road to Mohope Moor, with views of West Allendale. One mile from Ninebanks Village.
Facilities:	Room: 🛏,🖳 General: ⊁📶🗙🅰🐾♨🖥

MORPETH

Newminster Cottage ★★B&B

High Stanners, Morpeth, Northumberland, NE61 1QL

T:	+44 (0) 1670 503124
E:	enquiries@newminster-cottage.co.uk
W:	newminster-cottage.co.uk
Bedrooms:	3 • sleeps 6
Prices:	Double: £25-£35 per person per night breakfast included
Open:	Year round except Christmas and New Year
Description:	Beautiful 19thC cottage, idyllic riverside location, spacious and comfortable en suite accommodation and a breakfast to really kick start your day.
Facilities:	Room: ⁵🗙📺🛜📶🖥📺🖳🕮 General: ⊁🗙🅰♨🔌 Leisure: 🚲

NEWBIGGIN-BY-THE-SEA

Seaton House ★★★B&B

20 Seaton Avenue, Newbiggin-By-The-Sea, Northumberland, NE64 6UX

T:	+44 (0) 1670 816057
Bedrooms:	4 • sleeps 6
Prices:	Double and single: £25-£28 per person per night breakfast included • Cheques/cash accepted
Open:	Year round except Christmas and New Year
Description:	Home-made teas, and a warm, friendly homely welcome await you in the beautiful old town of Newbiggin-by-the-Sea.
Facilities:	Room: ⬡✗⬇🛏️⬜📺🔧 General: ✗P⬡⬤✿🔨 Leisure: 🎿♪►

NEWBROUGH

Carr Edge Farm ★★★★Farmhouse

Newbrough, Hexham, Northumberland, NE47 5EA

T:	+44 (0) 1434 674788
E:	stay@carredge.co.uk
W:	carredge.co.uk
Bedrooms:	3 • sleeps 8
Prices:	Double: £28-£35 per person per night breakfast included
Open:	Year round
Description:	Enjoy warm farmhouse welcome. Recently converted self-contained wing. Spacious en suite bedrooms, guest lounge. Ideally situated in Hadrian's Wall Corridor.
Facilities:	Room: ⬡✗⬛⬇🛏️📺🔧 General: ✗P⬤✿🔨 Leisure: U🎿►

NEWBROUGH

Westfield B&B ♦♦♦♦Guest Accommodation

Newbrough, Hexham, Northumberland, NE47 5AR

T:	+44 (0) 1434 674241
E:	byhexham@aol.com
W:	westfieldbandb.co.uk
Bedrooms:	2 • sleeps 5
Prices:	Double: £30-£45 per person per night breakfast included Cheques/cash accepted
Open:	Year round
Description:	A 1920s stone-built house. Formerly the village shop. Wonderful views over open countryside, on the Stanegate Roman road.
Facilities:	Room: ⬡✗⬛⬇🛏️📺🔧 General: ✗P⬤✿ Leisure: U►

NORTH SUNDERLAND

Leeholme ★★B&B

93 Main Street, Seahouses, Northumberland, NE68 7TS

T:	+44 (0) 1665 720230
E:	Lisaevans67@tiscali.co.uk
Bedrooms:	3 • sleeps 6
Prices:	Double: £20-£30 per person per night breakfast included
Open:	Year round except Christmas and New Year
Description:	A warm welcome awaits you at this small, homely B&B. Five minutes' walk to Seahouses harbour and shops. Hearty breakfast assured.
Facilities:	Room: General: Leisure:

OLD BEWICK

Old Bewick Farmhouse ★★★★B&B

Old Bewick, Alnwick, Northumberland, NE66 4DZ

T:	+44 (0) 1668 217372
E:	oldbewickfarmhouse@aol.com
W:	oldbewick.co.uk
Bedrooms:	2 • sleeps 6
Prices:	Double: £25-£35 per person per night breakfast included
Open:	Year round
Description:	Georgian farmhouse nine miles north of Alnwick in north Northumberland, offering quality B&B. Close to many historic places and within easy reach of the Heritage Coast.
Facilities:	Room: General:

SEAHOUSES

Springhill Farm — Self Catering rating applied for

Springhill Farm, Seahouses, Northumberland, NE68 7UR

T:	+44 (0) 1665 721820
E:	enquiries@springhill-farm.co.uk
W:	springhill-farm.co.uk
Units:	6 • sleeps 33
Prices:	From £195-£1,600 per week • Debit/credit card, cheques/cash accepted
Open:	Year round except Christmas and New Year
Description:	Peacefully situated property, 0.5 miles from the beautiful coast of Northumberland. With panoramic views of the Farne Islands, Bamburgh Castle and Cheviot Hills.
Facilities:	Room: General: Leisure:

STOCKSFIELD

Locksley B&B
♦♦♦♦Guest Accommodation

45 Meadowfield Road, Stocksfield, Northumberland, NE43 7PY   SILVER AWARD

T:	+44 (0) 1661 844778
E:	Josie@locksleybedandbreakfast co.uk
W:	locksleybedandbreakfast co.uk
Bedrooms:	3 • sleeps 6
Prices:	Double: £27.50 per person per night breakfast included Debit/credit card accepted
Open:	Year round
Description:	Well-appointed, comfortable family home set in beautiful gardens. Plenty of off-road parking, three rooms available, warm welcome awaits.
Facilities:	Room: ⚂✕⌷☎🕯📖📺📡 General: 🔌P🚭✕☼🍴 Leisure: ⚑

ULGHAM

The Carriage House
★★★★★Self Catering

The Old Vicarage, Ulgham Village, Morpeth, NE61 3AR

T:	+44 (0) 1670 790225
E:	joe@ulgham.demon.co.uk
W:	ulgham.demon.co.uk
Units:	1 • sleeps 5
Prices:	From £255-£495 per week • Cheques/cash accepted
Open:	Year round
Description:	Luxurious, newly renovated former carriage house to the vicarage. Superbly equipped, two en suite bedrooms, Jacuzzi, very comfortable beds. Close to Druridge Bay and Alnwick Castle.
Facilities:	Room: 📖 General: P📖🚭☼📡 Leisure: ∪🎣🚲⚑

WALL

Kiln Rigg
★★★zzSelf Catering

High Brunton, Hexham, Northumberland, NE46 4EQ

T:	+44 (0) 1434 681018
E:	kilnrigg@beeb.net
Units:	2 • sleeps 3
Prices:	From £185-£420 per week
Open:	Year round except Christmas and New Year
Description:	Situated on the edge of Hadrian's Wall this 18thC stone Bothy provides convenient access to Hexham, Corbridge and surrounding areas.
Facilities:	General: P☼📡

WARK

The Black Bull ★★★Inn

Wark, Hexham, Northumberland, NE48 3LG

T:	+44 (0) 1434 230239
W:	blackbullwark.co.uk
Bedrooms:	5 • sleeps 11
Prices:	Double: £25-£35 per person per night breakfast included Debit/credit card accepted
Open:	Year round
Description:	A warm welcome awaits visitors to this traditional country pub with restaurant facilities and beautifully appointed accommodation.
Facilities:	Room: ᵇ✕◻️🔥🔟,📺🛏️🕾 General: P◻️🍽️✕🅰️🚐✕❄️

WARKWORTH

Rebecca House ★★★★★Self Catering

25 Greens Park, Warkworth, Morpeth, NE65 0UP

T:	+44 (0) 1665 713118
E:	suefenlon@hotmail.com
W:	rebeccahouse.co.uk
Units:	1 • sleeps 6
Prices:	From £325-£725 per week
Open:	Year round except Christmas and New Year
Description:	Situated next to the River Coquet, Warkworth Castle and beach. The house has three double bedrooms all en suite, lounge, kitchen and garden. Sleeps six.
Facilities:	Room: 🛏️ General: P✕🅰️❄️▢ Leisure: ▶

WARKWORTH

West View Lodge ★★★★B&B

35 Watershaugh Road, Warkworth, Northumberland, NE65 0TX

T:	+44 (0) 1665 711532
E:	smgunn@aol.com
Bedrooms:	3 • sleeps 6
Prices:	Double: £22-£26 per person per night breakfast included Euros accepted
Open:	Year round except Christmas and New Year
Description:	West View is a large, attractive stone-built house with delightful views and a sunny, private garden.
Facilities:	Room: ◻️🔥🔟,📺▢🕾 General: ✕❄️🅰️ Leisure: ∪🚴♪▶

WHITFIELD

West Steel ♦♦♦ Guest Accommodation

Whitfield, Hexham, Northumberland, NE47 8JE

T:	+44 (0) 1434 344096
E:	a.dacosta@ukonline.co.uk
Bedrooms:	3 • sleeps 6
Prices:	Double: £22.50-£32.50 per person per night breakfast included
	Euros accepted
Open:	Year round
Description:	B&B accommodation available in a comfortable, relaxed environment situated on a working hill farm, fabulous views of Allen Valley.
Facilities:	Room: ⌖✕⬛✦▥⬛⬛⬛
	General: ✕P⬛⬛⬛⬛

WOOLER

Peth Head Cottage ★★★★ Self Catering

Booking address: Peth Head Cottage, 32 Kendor Grove, Morpeth, NE61 2BU

T:	+44 (0) 1670 514900
E:	peter@pncjeffreys.freeserve.co.uk
W:	pethheadcottage.co.uk
Units:	1 • sleeps 4
Prices:	From £195-£415 per week
Open:	Year round except Christmas and New Year
Description:	Peth Head Cottage provides high quality accommodation in Wooler, close to Northumberland's coast and castles, National Park and the Scottish Borders.
Facilities:	General: ⬛⬛⬛

WOOLER

Swallowfields Country Cottage ★★★★ Self Catering

Coldmartin, Alnwick and Berwick Countryside, Wooler NE71 6QN

T:	+44 (0) 1668 283488
E:	stay@coldmartin.co.uk
W:	coldmartin.co.uk
Units:	1 • sleeps 12
Prices:	From £350-£995 per week • Euros accepted
Open:	Year round
Description:	Spacious cottage with ground floor en suite accommodation. Surrounded by miles of fabulous walking, cycling, bird watching and star gazing.
Facilities:	Room: ▥
	General: P⬛⬛⬛
	Leisure: ⬛⬛

WOOLER

Tallet Country B&B   ◆◆◆◆◆ Guest Accommodation

Tallet, Alnwick, Northumberland, NE71 6QN   GOLD AWARD

T:	+44 (0) 1668 283488
E:	stay@coldmartin.co.uk
W:	coldmartin.co.uk
Bedrooms:	2 • sleeps 4
Prices:	Double: £30-£35 per person per night breakfast included
Open:	Year round except Christmas and New Year
Description:	Home-from-home comforts and most delicious breakfasts. We invite you to enjoy this special place. You will be most welcome.
Facilities:	Room: ♨✕◳⛊▥▤.⊞◹ General: ⑂P◳♨☼✲◳ Leisure: ♺♪

WOOLER

Tilldale House   ◆◆◆◆ Guest Accommodation

34/40 High Street, Wooler, Northumberland, NE71 6BG

T:	+44 (0) 1668 281450
E:	tilldalehouse@freezone.co.uk
Bedrooms:	3 • sleeps 6
Prices:	Double: £23-£26 per person per night breakfast included Cheques/cash accepted
Open:	Year round
Description:	Centrally situated in Wooler, 300-year-old, stone-built property having once been a small holding. Now with all modern comforts. Evening meal available on request. Non-smoking property.
Facilities:	Room: ♨✕◳⛊▥.⊞◹ General: ⑂◳♨◳ Leisure: ∪♺♪♪

BARNBY

Ivy Farm B&B   ◆◆◆ Guest Accommodation

Newark Road, Barnby in the Willows, Nottingham, Nottinghamshire, NG24 2SL

T:	+44 (0) 1636 672568
E:	clare@ivyfarm.f9.co.uk
W:	ivyfarm.f9.co.uk
Bedrooms:	5
Prices:	Double: £43 per room per night breakfast included
Open:	Year round
Description:	Comfortable B&B at a family farm location three miles east of the historic market town of Newark, only a few minutes from Newark Showground. Easy access from the main A1 trunk road and the A17 east coast road.
Facilities:	Room: ⊟ General: ⑂

BANBURY

Number 63
★★★★ Guesthouse

63 Oxford Road, Banbury, Oxfordshire, OX16 9AJ

T:	+44 (0) 1295 268396
E:	info@number-63.co.uk
W:	number-63.co.uk
Bedrooms:	3 • sleeps 7
Prices:	Double: £35-£55 per room per night breakfast included
Open:	Year round
Description:	Small, friendly B&B only a short walk to the town centre. Well-equipped, comfortable and spacious rooms, personal attention assured. Fax and wireless broadband facilities available.
Facilities:	Room: 🛏✕◻♨▥.📺☐📶 General: ✂🅿☕♨⚲✳

COTTISFORD

Manor Grange
★★★★ B&B

Manor Grange, Cottisford, Brackley, Oxfordshire, NN13 5SW

T:	+44 (0) 1280 847770
E:	triciahazan@aol.com
W:	manor-grange.com
Bedrooms:	2 • sleeps 4
Prices:	Double: £58 per room per night breakfast included
Open:	Year round except Christmas and New Year
Description:	Comfortable en suite rooms in a peaceful rural setting. Delicious home-cooked breakfasts with home made preserves. Less than 15 minutes to Silverstone racing circuit. Personal service from the friendly owners.
Facilities:	Call for details

FULBROOK

Star Cottage
◆◆◆ Guest Accommodation

Meadow Lane, Fulbrook, Burford, Oxfordshire, OX18 4BW   SILVER AWARD

T:	+44 (0) 1993 822032
E:	peterwyatt@tesco.net
Bedrooms:	1 • sleeps 3
Prices:	Double: £45-£75per room per night breakfast included Euros accepted
Open:	Year round
Description:	Georgian cottage with en suite spacious bedroom and downstairs stone floor breakfast room with open fire.
Facilities:	Room: 🛏✕◻♨✆📺📶 General: ☕♨⚲✳📺

LONG WITTENHAM

The Grange ★★★B&B

High Street, Long Wittenham, Abingdon, Oxfordshire, OX14 4QH

T:	+44 (0) 1865 407808
E:	grahamneil@talk21.com
W:	smoothhound.co.uk/hotels/grange5.html
Bedrooms:	3 • sleeps 6
Prices:	Double: £55 per room per night breakfast included
Open:	Year round
Description:	Spacious, Grade II Listed Georgian family house in picturesque riverside village. Set in 0.75 acre garden. Close to Abingdon, Didcot, Oxford and Wallingford. Excellent village pubs with good food.
Facilities:	Room: ⏚✕♨🖥️📺 General: ✕☺❄ Leisure: ∪♪▶

MILTON COMMON

Byways ♦♦♦♦Guest Accommodation

Old London Road, Milton Common, Thame, Oxfordshire, OX9 2JR

T:	+44 (0) 1844 279386
W:	bywaysbedandbreakfast.co.uk
Bedrooms:	3 • sleeps 5
Prices:	Double: £30-£35; Single: £35; both per person per night breakfast included • Cheques/cash accepted
Open:	Year round
Description:	Ground floor accommodation with views over open farmland. Welcoming with homely atmosphere. Emphasis on comfort and home cooking. Close to Ridgeway path, Oxfordshire cycleway and two golf courses.
Facilities:	Room: ⏚✕🖃♨🖥️🖐️ General: ✕🛄♨☺❄🅿️ Leisure: ▶

OLD MARSTON

Cherbridge Cottage ★★★★★Self Catering

Booking address: Hill Farm, Mill Lane, Marston, OX3 0QG

T:	+44 (0) 7976 288329
E:	enquiries@cherbridgecottages.co.uk
W:	cherbridgecottages.co.uk
Units:	1 • sleeps 5
Prices:	From £783 per week • Debit/credit card, euros accepted
Open:	Year round
Description:	Cherbridge Cottage is part of a 1930s punting station providing contemporary holiday accommodation. The property is set in large, secluded gardens with extensive river frontage, but only two miles from the centre of Oxford.
Facilities:	Room: 🖥️ General: ☺🎄❄🖵 Leisure: ∪🚲♪

OXFORD

Brenal Guesthouse ★★★ Guesthouse

307 Iffley Road, Oxford, Oxfordshire, OX4 4AG

T:	+44 (0) 1865 721561
E:	brenalguesthouse@hotmail.co.uk
Bedrooms:	5 • sleeps 11
Prices:	Double: £30-£35; Single: £30-40; both per person per night breakfast included • Debit/credit card, cheques/cash accepted
Open:	Year round
Description:	Welcoming warm and clean family-run guesthouse. Convenient to city centre and the ring road. River walks nearby. En suite rooms with TV and tea facilities. Car park, non-smoking establishment.
Facilities:	Room: ⱶ✕ⴱ🔲📺🔲🔲🔾 General: ✕P🔲🔾🔾🔾

SHIPTON-UNDER-WYCHWOOD

Plum Cottage ★★★★ Self Catering

Booking address: Manor Cottages & Cotswold Retreats,
Priory Mews, 33A Priory Lane, Burford, OX18 4SG

T:	+44 (0) 1993 824252
E:	mancott@netcomuk.co.uk
W:	geocities.com/plumcottage_shipton
Units:	1 • sleeps 6
Prices:	From £420-£620 per week • Debit/credit card, cheques/cash accepted
Open:	Year round
Description:	Plum Cottage is a ground floor converted barn sleeping five-six guests. Very private situation with views across open fields.
Facilities:	Room: 🔲 General: P🔲🔾🔾🔾🔾

STOKE LYNE

Stoke Lyne Farm Cottages ★★★★ Self Catering

Lower Farm, Bicester, Oxfordshire OX27 8SD

T:	+44 (0) 1869 345306
E:	info@stokelynefarmcottages.co.uk
W:	stokelynefarmcottages.co.uk
Units:	3 • sleeps 6
Prices:	From £285-£365 per week
Open:	Year round except Christmas and New Year
Description:	Two beautiful cottages on a family farm, converted from old stables with original features. In a quiet rural location.
Facilities:	General: P🔾🔾 Leisure: ∪🔾🔾🔾🔾

WATCHFIELD

The Coach House ★★★★Self Catering

Booking address: Cottage in the Country Cottage Holidays,
Forest Gate, Frog Lane, OX7 6JZ

T:	+44 (0) 1993 831495
E:	info@cottageinthecountry.co.uk
Units:	1 • sleeps 5
Prices:	From £270-£420 per week • Cheques/cash accepted
Open:	Year round except Christmas and New Year
Description:	Old Westmill Farmhouse and separate coach house are both Grade II Listed buildings, set in large gardens, mainly lawns and mature trees. Close to river and farmland.
Facilities:	General: P♿✿🖳

MANTON

Broccoli Bottom ★★★★B&B
SILVER AWARD

Wing Road, Manton, Oakham, LE15 8SZ

T:	07702 437102
E:	sally@udale.wanadoo.co.uk
Bedrooms:	2 • sleeps 4
Prices:	Double: £45 per person per night breakfast included
Open:	Year round
Description:	A renovated farmhouse set in seven acres. Situated in open countryside.
Facilities:	Call for details

BISHOPS CASTLE

Mount Cottage ★★★★Self Catering

The Mount, Bull Lane, Bishop's Castle, Shropshire, SY9 5DA

T:	+44 (0) 1588 638288
E:	heather@mountcottage.co.uk
W:	mountcottage.co.uk
Units:	1 • sleeps 4
Prices:	From £195-£320 per week
Open:	Year round
Description:	Cosy cottage with south-facing, walled garden. Beautifully converted and equipped from 17thC stone barn. Short walk from flourishing market town.
Facilities:	General: P♿✿🖳🖳

BITTERLEY

Angel Barn ★★★★ Self Catering

Booking address: Angel Gardens, Springfield, Bitterley, Shropshire, SY8 3HZ

T:	+44 (0) 1584 890381
E:	angelgardens@sy83hz.fsnet.co.uk
W:	stmem.com/angelbarn
Units:	1 • sleeps 2
Prices:	From £250-£378 per week
Open:	Year round
Description:	Ludlow seven minutes. Idyllic stone cottage at 1,000 feet. Breathtaking landscape views. Luxuriously appointed. Peaceful location in spectacular Angel Gardens. Tennis. Country pub/restaurant walkable.
Facilities:	General: **P⚡✿🖳** Leisure: ⚡

BROSELEY

The Old Rectory ◆◆◆◆◆ Guest Accommodation

46 Ironbridge Road, Broseley, Shropshire, TF12 5AF   SILVER AWARD

T:	+44 (0) 1952 883399
E:	info@theoldrectoryatbroseley.co.uk
W:	theoldrectoryatbroseley.co.uk
Bedrooms:	10 • sleeps 23
Prices:	Double: £49.95-£89.95 per room per night breakfast included Debit/credit card, cheques/cash accepted
Open:	Year round except Christmas and New Year
Description:	The Old Rectory is tranquilly set in two acres of established gardens and has recently been tastefully restored to very high standards.
Facilities:	Room: **◨☀🖵🛍.📺🖵🖳** General: **✂P⚡✿**

BUCKNELL

The Willows ★★★★ B&B

Bucknell, Craven Arms, Shropshire, SY7 0AA

T:	+44 (0) 1547 530201
E:	the_willows@btinternet.com
W:	willows-bucknell.co.uk
Bedrooms:	3 • sleeps 7
Prices:	Double: £25-27.50 per person per night breakfast include Debit/credit card accepted
Open:	Year round
Description:	15thC cruck house in peaceful village. Exposed beams, antique furnishings, period fireplaces. Hearty breakfasts from local produce. Library and games room. Tea rooms. Large topiary gardens.
Facilities:	Room: **◨☀🖵.📺🖵** General: **✂P🏠♨✿🖳** Leisure: **🚴♪⚑**

BURLTON

Greystones Barn Annexe ★★★ Self Catering

Greystones Barn, Petton, Burford, Shropshire, SY4 5TH

T:	+44 (0) 1939 270999
E:	kotti@btinternet.com
Units:	1 • sleeps 4
Prices:	From £200-£300 per week
Open:	Year round
Description:	Self-contained ground floor barn conversion annexe. Large living space, double bedroom, en suite shower room, sleeps two + two.
Facilities:	General:P⚅✿🖳

CHELMARSH

Bulls Head Inn ★★★ Self Catering

Chelmarsh, Bridgnorth, Shropshire, WV16 6BA

T:	+44 (0) 1746 861469
E:	bull_chelmarsh@btconnect.com
W:	bullsheadchelmarsh.co.uk
Units:	1 • sleeps 7
Prices:	From £230-£480 per week • Debit/credit card accepted
Open:	Year round
Description:	Superbly furnished cottage with stone featured walls. Sleeps seven adults/fully equipped. Quiet location near owners' 17thC inn.
Facilities:	General:🍽⚅✿🖳 Leisure: 🚲

CHURCH STRETTON

The Garden Flat ★★★ Self Catering

Ashfield House, Windle Hill, Church Stretton, Shropshire, SY6 7AP

T:	+44 (0) 1694 723715
E:	cj.hembrow@ukonline.co.uk
W:	thegardenflatchurchstretton.co.uk
Units:	1 • sleeps 2
Prices:	From £170-£200 per week
Open:	Year round
Description:	Cosy, modern ground floor flat in beautiful surroundings. Perfect base for walking/exploring. Town centre 10 miles walk. Sky TV. Parking. Garden. Warm welcome assured.
Facilities:	Room: 📺 General: P⚅✿📶🖳

SHROPSHIRE

CHURCH STRETTON

Victoria House   ★★★★Guest Accommodation
48 High Street, Church Stretton, Shropshire, SY6 6BX

T:	+44 (0) 1694 723823
E:	victoriahouse@fsmail.net
W:	bedandbreakfast-shropshire.co.uk
Bedrooms:	4 • sleeps 8
Prices:	Double: £22.50 per person per night breakfast included Euros accepted
Open:	Year round
Description:	Beautiful Victorian B&B in Church Stretton centre. All rooms individually staged period furniture and luxury finishing touches. Local produce, excellent breakfasts.
Facilities:	Room: ⍻✕◫⬙▥⃘.TV⍥ General: ⌇⌗♙

CLUN

The White Horse Inn   ★★★Inn
The Square, Clun, Shropshire, SY7 8JA

T:	+44 (0) 1588 640305
E:	jack@whi-clun.co.uk
W:	whi-clun.co.uk
Bedrooms:	4 • sleeps 11
Prices:	Double: £25-£32.50 per person per night breakfast included Debit/credit card accepted
Open:	Year round
Description:	A characterful, friendly and comfortable inn in the old market square at the centre of Clun. Ideal for walkers, cyclists and those just wanting a relaxing break in this peaceful area.
Facilities:	Room: ⍻✕◫⬙▥⃘.TV⍥ General: ⌗♙✕⌗⬚✕♫ Leisure: ✦

COALPORT

Ironbridge Youth Hostel (YHA)   ★★Hostel
John Rose Building, High Street, Telford, TF8 7HT

T:	+44 (0) 1952 588755
E:	ironbridge@yha.org.uk
W:	yha.org.uk
Dormitories:	25 • sleeps 92
Prices:	Dormitory pricing: £10.95-£15.50 • Debit/credit card, cheques/cash accepted
Open:	Year round
Description:	Two site youth hostel set within walking distance of the 10 industrial heritage museums. Hostel offers excellent quality accommodation and meals at budget prices.
Facilities:	Room: ▥⃘.TV General: ⌗P⬚⌗✕✕♙ Leisure: ⛓✦

COALPORT

Station House Holiday Lets ★★★★ Self Catering

Station House, Coalport, Shropshire, TF8 7JF

T:	+44 (0) 1952 881106
E:	enquiries@coalportstation.com
W:	coalportstation.com
Units:	1 • sleeps 4
Prices:	From £349-£695 per week • Euros accepted
Open:	Year round
Description:	A renovated railway carriage offering all modern luxuries in a former country station setting. Away from it all, near the river.
Facilities:	General: P✂❄▣ Leisure: ᕫ♿♪►

ELLERDINE

1 Oak House Farm Cottages ★★★★ Self Catering

Booking address: 1 Hewitt Street, Northwich, CW9 7TR

T:	+44 (0) 1606 351521
E:	info@yourshropshirecottage.co.uk
W:	yourshropshirecottage.co.uk
Units:	1 • sleeps 5
Prices:	From £190 per week
Open:	Year round
Description:	Charming 18thC cottage set within a working arable farm. Comfortable and well equipped. Includes inglenook with wood burning stove.
Facilities:	General: P✂❄▣

FISHMORE

Elm Lodge B&B ★★★★ B&B

Elm Lodge, Fishmore, Ludlow, Shropshire, SY8 3DP

T:	+44 (0) 1584 872308
E:	info@elm-lodge.org.uk
W:	elm-lodge.org.uk
Bedrooms:	3 • sleeps 6
Prices:	Double: £25-£27.50 per person per night breakfast included Debit/credit card, euros accepted
Open:	Year round
Description:	Elm Lodge & Golf Course is a mile from the centre of the historic town of Ludlow, in a rural setting near a bus and train station. Cycle hire and walks.
Facilities:	Room: ♨✆▥📺🍵♿ General: ✄P✂❄ Leisure: ♿►

IRONBRIDGE

Woodville B&B ★★★B&B

4A The Woodlands, Ironbridge, TF8 7PA

T:	+44 (0) 1952 433343
E:	foxpeter3@aol.com
Bedrooms:	4 • sleeps 8
Prices:	Double: £40-£50; Single: £30-£35; both per room per night breakfast included
Open:	Year round
Description:	Long Distance Paths of Shropshire Way and Monarch's Way are nearby. Lifts to and from the footpaths available by arrangement. Dogs allowed. A non-smoking establishment.
Facilities:	Room: 🖃✕🛈🏧📺🕭 General: ✕P✕🌣🐾

LONGVILLE

Wilderhope Manor YHA ★★Hostel

The John Cadbury Memorial Hostel, Much Wenlock, Shropshire, TF13 6EG

T:	0870 770 6090
E:	wilderhope@yha.org.uk
W:	yha.org.uk
Dormitories:	9 • sleeps 54
Prices:	Dormitory pricing: £9-£12.50 • Debit/credit card, cheques/cash accepted
Open:	Year round
Description:	A 16thC manor house with modern and comfortable facilities. Leased from the National Trust.
Facilities:	Room: 🖃✕🛈🏧📺 General: ✕P🖃✕🚌✕🖳🖳📠 Leisure: ∪🐾🎣

MARKET DRAYTON

The Hermitage ◆◆◆◆Guest Accommodation

44 Stafford Street, Market Drayton, Shropshire, TF9 1JB

T:	+44 (0) 1630 658508
E:	info@thehermitagebb.co.uk
W:	thehermitagebb.co.uk
Bedrooms:	4 • sleeps 8
Prices:	Double: £25-£30 per person per night breakfast included
Open:	Year round
Description:	A large Victorian house offering a quality environment for holidays or business, set in the pretty market town of Market Drayton.
Facilities:	Room: 🖃✕🛈🏧📺🕭 General: ✕♨✕🖳

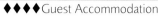

NEEN SOLLARS

Hop Barn
★★★★Self Catering

Neen Court, Neen Sollars, Kidderminster, Shropshire, DY14 0AH

T:	+44 (0) 1299 271204
E:	birgit.jones@onetel.net
Units:	1 • sleeps 4
Prices:	From £220-£360 per week • Euros accepted
Open:	Year round
Description:	A detached mellow brick cottage converted from outbuildings which pre-date the owners' Victorian house in a small village on quiet lanes.
Facilities:	General: P⚹⚹🖳

ONIBURY

Upper Onibury Cottages
★★★★Self Catering

Upper Onibury, Craven Arms, Shropshire, SY7 9AW

T:	+44 (0) 1584 856206
E:	info@shropshirecottages.com
W:	shropshirecottages.com
Units:	4 • sleeps 26
Prices:	From £250-£400 per week
Open:	Year round
Description:	Upper Onibury Cottages offer luxurious self-catering accommodation in rural south Shropshire, near to the ancient market town of Ludlow.
Facilities:	General: P⚹⚹🔲🖳 Leisure: ⚓⚹🏹

RATLINGHOPE

Bridges Youth Hostel (Long Mynd)
★Hostel

Ratlinghope, Shrewsbury, Shropshire, SY5 0SP

T:	+44 (0) 1588 650656
W:	yha.org.uk
Dormitories:	5 • sleeps 30
Prices:	Dormitory pricing: £7-£10 • Cheques/cash accepted
Open:	Year round
Description:	Converted school in the heart of the Shropshire hills. Rich in wildlife, superb walking/cycling. Open moorland, scenic valleys. Homemade food available. Camping. Advance bookings only.
Facilities:	Room: ⚹🎸📺 General: P⚹⚹🚐✕🎸 Leisure: U🚵

STANTON LACY

Sutton Court Farm Cottages ★★★★ Self Catering

Little Sutton, Stanton Lacy, Ludlow, Shropshire, SY8 2AJ

T:	+44 (0) 1584 861305
E:	enquiries@suttoncourtfarm.co.uk
W:	suttoncourtfarm.co.uk
Units:	6 • sleeps 20
Prices:	From £200-£500 per week • Cheques/cash accepted
Open:	Year round
Description:	Six special cottages set around a peaceful, rural courtyard in the Corvedale. Five miles from Ludlow. Cream teas and evening meals by arrangement. B&B also available.
Facilities:	General: **P**⚡✿🔌💻

TUGFORD

Tugford Farm B&B ♦♦♦ Guest Accommodation

Tugford Farm, Craven Arms, Shropshire, SY7 9HS

T:	+44 (0) 1584 841259
E:	williamstugford@supanet.com
W:	tugford.com
Bedrooms:	4 • sleeps 9
Prices:	Double: £30-£35 per person per night breakfast included Debit/credit card accepted
Open:	Year round
Description:	Top quality accommodation deep in the Corvedale Valley. En suite, central heating. Hearty farmhouse breakfast Ideal walking, cycling, riding. Central location for touring.
Facilities:	Room: ▯⚡▥📺🔌 General: ✂**P**⚡🚐✗ Leisure: ♅

BATCOMBE

The Coach House at Boords Farm ★★★★ Self Catering

Boords Farm, Batcombe, Shepton Mallet, Somerset, BA4 6HD

T:	+44 (0) 1749 850372
E:	info@boordsfarm.co.uk
W:	boordsfarm.co.uk
Units:	1 • sleeps 4
Prices:	From £375-£450 per week • Euros accepted
Open:	Year round
Description:	Recently converted coach house in grounds of 16thC thatched farmhouse. Equipped to high standard, providing very comfortable accommodation. Beautiful rural setting.
Facilities:	General: **P**⚡✿🔌 Leisure: ⚡🎾↾

* For details on accessible ratings, please visit enjoyengland.com/quality.

BATH

Forum Square ★★★★ Self Catering

Booking address: The Brow, Church Road, Combe Down, Bath BA2 5JL

T:	+44 (0) 1225 833314
E:	sue.forum@btinternet.com
W:	bathholidayhome.com
Units:	1 • sleeps up to 6
Prices:	From £375-£750 per week
Open:	Year round except Christmas and New Year
Description:	Elegant, Georgian-style townhouse in World Heritage city of Bath; two-six guests; four bedrooms; private garden; garage and parking space.
Facilities:	General: P✗✿▤

BATHEALTON

Hagley Bridge Farm ★★★★ Farmhouse

Hagley Bridge Farm, Taunton, Somerset, TA4 2BQ

T:	+44 (0) 1984 629026
Bedrooms:	2 • sleeps 4
Prices:	Double: £30-£35 per person per night breakfast included
Open:	Year round
Description:	Charming Somerset longhouse, by river in beautiful valley. Secluded, peaceful, but within easy reach of South West's many attractions.
Facilities:	Room: ⊱✗♨▥TV♨, General: P♨✗✿ Leisure: ♪⊦

BATHEASTON

Avondale Riverside Self Catering rating applied for

Booking address: 104 Lower Northend, North End, Batheaston, Bath, BA1 7HA

T:	+44 (0) 1225 852226
E:	sheilapex@questmusic.co.uk
W:	riversapart.co.uk
Units:	2 • sleeps 8
Prices:	From £490-£612 per week • Euros accepted
Open:	Year round except Christmas and New Year
Description:	Two balconied riverside apartments overlooking nature reserve. Private garden, secure parking, widescreen TV, whirlpool bath, en suite bedrooms. Ten minute drive to city centre.
Facilities:	Room: TV General: P✗✿▤ Leisure: U♨♪

BILBROOK

Steps Farmhouse  ◆◆◆◆ Guest Accommodation

Bilbrook, Minehead, Somerset, TA24 6HE

T:	+44 (0) 1984 640974
E:	info@stepsfarmhouse.co.uk
W:	stepsfarmhouse.co.uk
Bedrooms:	3 • sleeps 8
Prices:	Double: £22.50-£27.50 per person per night breakfast included Debit/credit card, euros accepted
Open:	Year round except Christmas and New Year
Description:	Traditional 16thC former farmhouse situated close to Dunster and Minehead, offering a selection of comfortable en suite B&B accommodation.
Facilities:	Room: ⁵⁄×⬜⬆▥,ⷮⴸ General:P✂✳ Leisure: ▶

BISHOP SUTTON

The Trebartha ★★★★ Self Catering

The Street, Bristol, BS39 5UU

T:	+44 (0) 1984 640974
W:	trebartha.co.uk
Units:	1 • sleeps 4
Prices:	From £330-£400 per week • Euros accepted
Open:	Year round
Description:	Well equipped annexe in peaceful countryside; wonderful views; ideal base walking, cycling, fishing and touring; 30 minutes from Bath, Bristol and Wells.
Facilities:	General: P✂✳⬜ Leisure: ⬢⬤

BREAN

The Old Rectory Motel ◆◆◆◆ Guest Accommodation

Church Road, Brean, Burnham-on-Sea, Somerset, TA8 2SF

T:	+44 (0) 1278 751447
E:	helen@old-rectory.fsbusiness.co.uk
W:	old-rectory.fsbusiness.co.uk
Bedrooms:	10 • sleeps 22
Prices:	Double: £22.50-£32.50; Single: £25-£40; both per person per night breakfast included • Debit/credit card accepted
Open:	Year round
Description:	Ground floor en suite accommodation suitable for all – converted from old carriage house and school room.
Facilities:	Room: ⁵⁄×⬜⬆▥,ⷮⴸ General: ▣✂▦✳▨ Leisure: ∪⬤▶

BRUSHFORD

Three Acres Country House ★★★★Guest Accom
Brushford, Dulverton, Somerset, TA22 9AR   SILVER AWARD

T:	+44 (0) 1398 323730
E:	enquiries@threeacrescountryhouse.co.uk
W:	threeacrescountryhouse.co.uk
Bedrooms:	6 • sleeps 14
Prices:	Double: £35-£65 per person per night room only Debit/credit card, cheques/cash accepted
Open:	Year round
Description:	Set in peaceful surroundings with relaxed atmosphere; breakfast at leisure; lounge; log fires; bar and sun terrace; luxury en suite rooms; 10% discount for a three or more night stay.
Facilities:	Room: ⁵⅝✕⊞♨☎▥⎕TV☜⋠ General: ▥♨⚑✗✿⌘ Leisure: ∪⤶

BUTCOMBE

Butcombe Farm ★★★★Guest Accommodation
Butcombe Farm, Aldwick Lane, Bristol, BS40 7UW

T:	+44 (0) 1761 462380
Bedrooms:	7 • sleeps 15
Prices:	Double: £50-£54; Single: £35-39; both per room per night room only • Debit/credit card accepted
Open:	Year round
Description:	Country farmhouse accommodation in Area of Outstanding Natural Beauty near Blagdon Lake at foot of Mendip Hills. Farm mentioned in Domesday Book, oldest part of house dates to late 14thC.
Facilities:	Room: ⁵⅝✕⊞♨☎▥⎕TV General: ♨✗✿⌘ Leisure: ∪⤶⚓⤷

CHEDDAR

Applebee South Barns B&B ★★Guest Accommodation
The Hayes, Cheddar, Somerset, BS27 3AN

T:	+44 (0) 1934 743146
Bedrooms:	8 • sleeps 16
Prices:	Double: £20-£24 per room per night room only
Open:	Year round except Christmas and New Year
Description:	Quiet, secluded converted stone barns in sun-trap gardens. A friendly relaxing atmosphere in centre of Cheddar Village with private parking.
Facilities:	Call for details

CHEDDAR

Spring Cottages ★★★★Self Catering

Spring Cottage, Venns Gate, Cheddar, Somerset, BS27 3LW

T:	+44 (0) 1934 742493
E:	buckland@springcottages.co.uk
Units:	3 • sleeps 6
Prices:	From £310 per week
Open:	Year round
Description:	A barn conversion into three comfortable and well-appointed cottages with attractive gardens. Ample parking.
Facilities:	Call for details

COCKLAKE

Cricklake Farm ♦♦♦Guest Accommodation

Cocklake, Wedmore, Somerset, BS28 4HH

T:	+44 (0) 1934 712736
Bedrooms:	3 • sleeps 7
Prices:	Double: £27.50-£30 per room per night room only Debit/credit card accepted
Open:	Year round
Description:	You can relax on our working dairy farm. An ideal place to stay, situated along the banks of the river Axe; a delightful area for walking and wildlife.
Facilities:	Room: ⬛✕⬛⬛⬛⬛⬛⬛ General: ⬛⬛⬛⬛

DUNSTER

Yarn Market Hotel (Exmoor) ★★★Hotel

5-33 High Street, Dunster, Minehead, Somerset, TA24 6SF

T:	+44 (0) 1643 821425
E:	yarnmarket.hotel@virgin.net
W:	yarnmarkethotel.co.uk
Bedrooms:	15 • sleeps 33
Prices:	Double: £30-£45; Single: £40-£55; both per person per night breakfast included • Debit/credit card, euros accepted
Open:	Year round
Description:	Central and accessible hotel in quaint English village, an ideal location from which to explore the Exmoor National Park.
Facilities:	Room: ⬛✕⬛⬛⬛⬛⬛⬛⬛ General: ⬛⬛⬛⬛⬛✕⬛ Leisure: ⬛⬛⬛

EXFORD

Exmoor White Horse Inn ★★★ Hotel

Exford, Exmoor National Park, Somerset, TA24 7PY

T:	+44 (0) 1643 831229
E:	info@exmoor-whitehorse.co.uk
W:	devon-hotels.co.uk

Bedrooms:	28 • sleeps 58
Prices:	Double and single £45 per person per night breakfast included Debit/credit card, cheques/cash accepted
Open:	Year round
Description:	16thC inn of character-log fires, oak beams. Traditional home-cooked food using local produce. Sumptuous en suite bedrooms.
Facilities:	Room: ⚅✕⌷🔌☎🖥📺📶 General: ⬜🅿♨✕🚍✕☀🅿 Leisure: ∪🏊

HILLCOMMON

Higher House ★★★ Self Catering

Hillcommon, Taunton, Somerset, TA4 1DU

T:	+44 (0) 1823 400570
E:	mail@higherhouse.co.uk
W:	higherhouse.co.uk

Units:	1 • sleeps 5
Prices:	From £205-£375 per week
Open:	Year round except Christmas and New Year
Description:	Excellent touring base, with easy access to the West Country's north and south coasts; wonderful landscaped gardens giving onto open countryside; ideal for walking, cycling, riding, golf, water sports and fishing.
Facilities:	Room: 🛏 General: 🅿♨🔥☀🖥 Leisure: ∪♿🏇♣

LOWER GODNEY

Double-Gate Farm ◆◆◆◆ Guest Accommodation

Godney, Wells, Somerset, BA5 1RX   GOLD AWARD

T:	+44 (0) 1458 832217
E:	doublegatefarm@aol.com
W:	doublegatefarm.com

Bedrooms:	6 • sleeps 14
Prices:	Double: £30-£35 per person per night breakfast included Debit/credit card accepted
Open:	Year round
Description:	Lovely Georgian farmhouse on working farm. Quality accommodation on a homely basis. Two golden retrievers and two loving moggies. Evening meals at village inn close by.
Facilities:	Room: ⚅✕🔌📺📶🖥 General: ✂🖥☎♨☀🅿 Leisure: ♣✦

LUCCOMBE

Wychanger
★★★★Self Catering

Luccombe, Wychanger, Minehead, Somerset, TA24 8TA

T:	+44 (0) 1643 862526
E:	holidays@wychanger.net
W:	wychanger.net
Units:	2 • sleeps 8
Prices:	From £325-£500 per week
Open:	Year round except Christmas and New Year
Description:	Two luxurious self-contained apartments in a converted coach house, set in spacious secluded grounds, with private access onto stunning Exmoor.
Facilities:	General: P🐾❄️🔲🗄️

MINEHEAD

The Parks Guesthouse
★★★★Guesthouse

26 The Parks, Minehead, Somerset, TA24 8BT
SILVER AWARD

T:	+44 (0) 1643 703547
E:	info@parksguesthouse.co.uk
W:	parksguesthouse.co.uk
Bedrooms:	7 • sleeps 20
Prices:	Double: £26-£29.50 per person per night breakfast included Debit/credit card, cheques/cash accepted
Open:	Year round except Christmas and New Year
Description:	Grade II Listed Georgian house full of charm, character and comfort. Ideally situated in lovely area between coast and Exmoor. Single occupancy rate for double/twin room is £35.
Facilities:	Room: 🔲🛁🔲📺🔲 General: ✂️🐾❄️📮

NETHER STOWEY

Castle of Comfort
◆◆◆◆◆Guest Accommodation

Dodington, Nether Stowey, Bridgwater, Somerset, TA5 1LE
SILVER AWARD

T:	+44 (0) 1278 741264
E:	reception@castle-of-comfort.co.uk
W:	castle-of-comfort.co.uk
Bedrooms:	6 • sleeps 13
Prices:	Double: £95-£129; Single: £38; both per room per night breakfast included • Debit/credit card, euros accepted
Open:	Year round
Description:	Small 16thC country house hotel nestling in Quantock Hills with views over the Bristol Channel.
Facilities:	Room: 🛏️✖️🔲🛁📞🔲📺🔲 General: ✂️📮✖️❄️📮 Leisure: ↺🎵🏹

PENSFORD

Greenacres (Stanton Wick) ★★Guest Accommodation

Stanton Wick, Bristol, BS39 4BX

T:	+44 (0) 1761 490397
Bedrooms:	6 • sleeps 12
Prices:	Double: £48-£90; Single: £25-£30; both per room per night breakfast included
Open:	Year round except Christmas and New Year
Description:	A friendly welcome awaits in peaceful setting, off A37. Relax and enjoy panoramic views across Chew Valley to Dundry Hills.
Facilities:	Room: ⁹✖ⓦ▥.ⓉⓋ☜ General: ✏P✗❀◪ Leisure: ◗

PORLOCK

Exmoor House ★★★★★Guest Accommodation

Minehead Road, Porlock, Minehead, Somerset, TA24 8EY   SILVER AWARD

T:	+44 (0) 1643 863599
E:	ann@exmoor-house.co.uk
W:	exmoor-house.co.uk
Bedrooms:	3 • sleeps 5
Prices:	Double: £35; Single: £30; both per person per night breakfast included
Open:	Year round
Description:	Exmoor Excellence Award, Guest Accommodation of the Year 2006. Stunning Georgian-style house with spectacular views, comfortable beds and the warm welcome to make your stay special.
Facilities:	Room: ⁹✖Œⓦ▥.ⓉⓋ☜ General: ✏P♨✗❀◪ Leisure: Ü♣▶

WELLS

Shalom ★★Self Catering

Booking address: 60 Eastgrove Avenue, Sharples, Bolton, BL1 7HA

T:	+44 (0) 1204 418576
E:	rosey.rees@talk21.com
Units:	1 • sleeps 5
Prices:	From £140-£345 per week • Cheques/cash accepted
Open:	Year round
Description:	Peace and tranquillity welcome you at Shalom. Holiday bungalow with garden, trees and shrubs. Open all year. Sleeps five. City centre 10 minutes' walk.
Facilities:	General: P✗❀▦

WELLS

The Crown at Wells ★★Hotel

Market Place, Wells, Somerset, BA5 2RP

T:	+44 (0) 1749 673457
E:	stay@crownatwells.co.uk
W:	crownatwells.co.uk

Bedrooms:	15 • sleeps 30
Prices:	Double: £80-£100; Single: £60-£90; both per room per night breakfast included • Debit/credit card, cheques/cash accepted
Open:	Year round
Description:	15thC coaching inn overlooking the medieval market place, a short walk from Wells Cathedral and the Bishop's Palace.
Facilities:	Room: ⬛✕⬛⬛⬛⬛,ⓉⓋ⬛ General: P⬛⬛⬛⬛⬛✕♫☀⬛ Leisure: ▶

WEST LYDFORD

Fosse House Farm ♦♦♦Guest Accommodation

Lydford on Fosse, Somerton, Somerset, TA11 7DW

T:	+44 (0) 1963 240268
E:	parkhouse@fossehousefarm.co.uk
W:	fossehousefarm.co.uk

Bedrooms:	4 • sleeps 7
Prices:	Double: £25-£35; Single: £25-27.50; both per person per night breakfast included
Open:	Year round
Description:	Friendly comfortable accommodation awaits within seven acres, en suite rooms with TV and tea-making facilities; ideal touring base.
Facilities:	Room: ⬛✕⬛⬛⬛,ⓉⓋ⬛ General: ✕P⬛

WEST QUANTOXHEAD

Stilegate B&B ★★★★★Guest Accommodation

West Quantoxhead, Taunton, Somerset, TA4 4DN

T:	+44 (0) 1984 639119
E:	stilegate@aol.com
W:	stilegate.co.uk

Bedrooms:	3 • sleeps 6
Prices:	Double: £50-£70 per room per night breakfast included Debit/credit card, euros accepted
Open:	Year round
Description:	Award-winning B&B in area of Outstanding Natural Beauty overlooking Exmoor National Park. Disabled guests welcome (mobility level 1 2003 assessment by ETC).
Facilities:	Room: ⬛✕⬛⬛⬛,ⓉⓋ⬛ General: ✕P⬛⬛⬛☀⬛ Leisure: U♪▶

WRANTAGE

Meare Court Cottages — Self Catering rating applied for

Meare Court, Meare Green, Taunton, Somerset, TA3 6DA

T:	+44 (0) 1823 480570
E:	mearecourt@farming.co.uk
W:	mearecourt.co.uk
Units:	3 • sleeps 16
Prices:	From £170-£950 per week • Debit/credit card, cheques/cash accepted
Open:	Year round
Description:	Idyllic countryside surroundings. Converted barns retaining original features. Beautiful spa room with hot tub and sauna. Beauty therapies. Linen and towels included. Sleeps two-15.
Facilities:	General: P▣✄❄▣ Leisure: ∪♪►

BURNTWOOD

Davolls Cottage — ◆◆◆◆Guest Accommodation

Davolls Cottage, 156 Woodhouses Road, Burntwood, Staffordshire, WS7 9EL

T:	+44 (0) 1543 671250
Bedrooms:	3 • sleeps 8
Prices:	Double: £23-£30 per person per night breakfast included
Open:	Year round
Description:	Country cottage situated by woodland, with easy access to Lichfield and the surrounding areas. Privacy is assured at this quiet, comfortable accommodation, which includes guests' own lounge. Secure parking and friendly atmosphere.
Facilities:	Room: ▥ General: ⚲P❄▤

CALTON

Field Head Farm House Holidays ★★★★Self Catering

Booking address: Stoney Rock Farm, Waterhouses, ST10 3LH

T:	+44 (0) 1538 308352
E:	janet@field-head.co.uk
W:	field-head.co.uk
Units:	1 • sleeps 11
Prices:	From £565-£1,195 per week
Open:	Year round
Description:	Grade II Listed farmhouse, well equipped, Sky TV, close to Manifold Valley, Dovedale, Alton Towers 15-minute drive. Secluded location, beautiful area for the walker, cyclist, horse rider. All welcome.
Facilities:	Room: ☏▣ General: P❄ Leisure: ∪

ILAM

Throwley Hall Farm B&B ♦♦♦♦ Guest Accommodation

Throwley Hall Farm, Ilam, Ashbourne, Staffordshire, DE6 2BB

T:	+44 (0) 1538 308202
E:	throwleyhall@btinternet.com
W:	throwleyhallfarm.co.uk
Bedrooms:	4 • sleeps 10
Prices:	Double: £29-£32 per person per night breakfast included
Open:	Year round
Description:	Stay on a farm where cows and calves, sheep and lambs nurture alongside wildlife and flowers in spring and summer. Near Manifold Valley, Dovedale, Alton Towers, stately homes and the Potteries.
Facilities:	Room: 🖩 General: ⚲P☼🏴

PENKRIDGE

Dalraddy Cottage ★★★★ Self Catering

Broadhurst Green Road, Pottal Pool, Abbots Langley, Staffordshire, ST19 5RR

T:	+44 (0) 1785 715700
E:	sonia@adamsyoung.fsnet.co.uk
W:	dalraddycottage.co.uk
Units:	1 • sleeps 4
Prices:	From £150-£400 per week
Open:	Year round
Description:	A luxury, two-bedroomed detached bungalow on Cannock Chase, Staffordshire. Ideal for walkers and cyclists. Golf and pony trekking nearby.
Facilities:	General: ☼ Leisure: ∪►

SWINSCOE

The Dog and Partridge Country Inn ★★ Hotel

The Dog & Partridge Country Inn, Swinscoe, Ashbourne, Staffordshire, DE6 2HS

T:	+44 (0) 1335 343183
W:	dogandpartridge.co.uk
Bedrooms:	32 • sleeps 118
Prices:	Double: £37.50 per person per night breakfast included Debit/credit card accepted
Open:	Year round
Description:	Family-run traditional country inn with rooms in the grounds. Good food, real ales, children and pets welcome. Ideal base for Peak District. Alton Towers only 15 minutes away. It has a bar and a la carte food is served daily.
Facilities:	Room: 📺 General: 🍴✕☼ Leisure: ♠

TUTBURY

Woodhouse Farm B&B ◆◆◆Guest Accommodation
Fauld, Tutbury, Burton-on-Trent, Staffordshire, DE13 9HR

T:	+44 (0) 1283 812185
E:	woodhousetutbury@aol.com
W:	woodhousebandb.co.uk
Bedrooms:	4 • sleeps 10
Prices:	Double: £25-£30 per person per night breakfast included
Open:	Year round
Description:	Woodhouse Farm dates to the 12thC and has strong connections with the castle. It is part of the Duchy of Lancaster estate and has lovely rural views. Five minutes off the A50 Stoke-Nottingham road, ideal for business or holiday.
Facilities:	Room: 📖 General: ✂☼ Leisure: ↑

UPPER HULME

Hurdlow Cottage ★★★★Self Catering
Hurdlow Farm, Upper Hulme, Leek, Staffordshire, ST13 8TX

T:	+44 (0) 1538 300406
E:	robertruth@hurdlowfarm.fsnet.co.uk
W:	hurdlowfarm.fsnet.co.uk
Units:	1 • sleeps 6
Prices:	From £200-£450 per week
Open:	Year round
Description:	Hurdlow Cottage, an 18thC farmhouse set on a working family farm which boasts views of the Roaches and heather moorland.
Facilities:	General: P☼

WINKHILL

Country Cottage ◆◆◆◆Guest Accommodation
Country Cottage, Back Lane Farm, Leek, Staffordshire, ST13 7XZ

T:	+44 (0) 1538 308273
E:	mjb6435@bentleym.plus.com
W:	geocities.com/mengli_55427
Bedrooms:	4 • sleeps 7
Prices:	Double: £24.50; Single: £25.50; both per person per night breakfast included
Open:	Year round
Description:	Back Lane Farm is situated in the rural countryside, halfway between Leek and Ashbourne, on the southern edge of the Peak Park. It is the home of Menga and Michael Bentley. We offer peaceful surroundings, pleasant rooms and good food.
Facilities:	Room: 📺 General: ✂P(❚X☼

CRATFIELD

School Farm Cottages ★★★★Self Catering

Church Road, Cratfield, Halesworth, Suffolk, IP19 0BU

T:	+44 (0) 1986 798844
E:	schoolfarmcotts@aol.com
W:	schoolfarmcottages.com
Units:	4 • sleeps 12
Prices:	From £154-£203 per week
Open:	Year round
Description:	High quality self-catering accommodation in converted traditional buildings on our small working farm in beautiful, rolling countryside.
Facilities:	General: ✿ Leisure: ◉☀

DARSHAM

Granary and The Mallards ★★★★Self Catering

Priory Farm, Darsham, Suffolk, IP17 3QD

T:	+44 (0) 1728 668459
E:	suebloomfield@btconnect.com
W:	holidaysatprioryfarm.co.uk
Units:	2 • sleeps 6
Prices:	From £182-£231 per week
Open:	Year round
Description:	The Granary sleeps four and is on the first floor. The Mallards sleeps two and is on the ground floor (wheelchair friendly).
Facilities:	General: ✿ Leisure: ◉

EDWARDSTONE

Larch & Spruce Cottages ★★★Self Catering

The White Horse Inn, Mill Green, Edwardstone, CO10 5PX

T:	+44 (0) 1787 211211
E:	john.norton@nortonorganic.co.uk
W:	tiscover.co.uk/gb/guide/5gb,en/objectId,ACC38843gb/home.html
Units:	2 • sleeps 7
Prices:	From £175-£275 per week
Open:	Year round
Description:	The White Horse is a friendly pub on a quiet lane in the village of Edwardstone. The cottages are situated in a small field behind the pub.
Facilities:	General: ▼

FELIXSTOWE

The Grafton Guesthouse ◆◆◆◆ Guest Accommodation
13 Sea Road, Felixstowe, Suffolk, IP11 2BB

T:	+44 (0) 1394 284881
Bedrooms:	8 • sleeps 14
Prices:	Double: £40-£48 per room per night breakfast included Single: £23.50-£29.50 per person per night breakfast included • Cheques/cash accepted
Open:	Year round
Description:	Elegant seafront premises. Spacious, well presented and comfortable establishment.
Facilities:	Room: ♙✕⤓☰✆▥.TV🖉 General: ⚥☒

HADLEIGH

Angel Cottage ★★★★Self Catering
Booking address: Period Cottage Holidays Ltd,
Pipers Ley, Burstall Hill, Burstall, IP8 3ED

T:	+44 (0) 1473 652356
E:	nadia@periodcottageholidays.co.uk
W:	periodcottageholidays.co.uk
Units:	1 • sleeps 4
Prices:	From £250-£525 per week
Open:	Year round
Description:	Angel Cottage is a 16thC, Grade II Listed cottage, situated in the pretty Suffolk market town of Hadleigh.
Facilities:	General: ✿

HESSETT

Heathfield ★★★★Self Catering
Booking address: Arcadia, Bury St Edmunds, IP30 9AB

T:	+44 (0) 1359 271130
E:	chriswhitton@aol.com
W:	tiscover.co.uk/gb/guide/5gb,en/objectId,ACC16170gb/home.html
Units:	1 • sleeps 4
Prices:	From £280-£385 per week
Open:	Year round
Description:	This pleasant, comfortable bungalow is on the edge of the quiet village of Hessett. Only two miles from the A14 and close to historic Bury St Edmunds.
Facilities:	General: ✿

LOWESTOFT

Banner Court 10   ★★★Self Catering

32A Kirkley Cliff Road, Lowestoft, Suffolk, NR33 0DB

T:	+44 (0) 1502 511876
E:	aishakhalaf@hotmail.com
W:	tiscover.co.uk/gb/guide/5gb,en/objectId,ACC17017gb/home.html
Units:	1 • sleeps 4
Prices:	From £455 per week
Open:	Year round
Description:	Two-bedroomed ground floor flat with small patio and garden. Large, elegant rooms, recently refurbished and furnished. Five minutes from beach and gardens. A 15 minute walk along promenade into town.
Facilities:	General: ✿

STRATFORD ST ANDREW

Toad Hall Flat   ★★★Self Catering

Toad Hall Flat, Stratford St Andrew, Suffolk, IP17 1LJ

T:	+44 (0) 1728 603463
E:	perryhunt@keme.co.uk
W:	tiscover.co.uk/gb/guide/5gb,en/objectId,ACC16706gb/home.html
Units:	1 • sleeps 2
Prices:	From £254 per week
Open:	Year round
Description:	A spacious first floor studio flat, ideal for two people, located within easy reach of Aldeburgh, Orford, Snape and Dunwich.
Facilities:	Call for details

WALDRINGFIELD

Quayside Cottage   ★★★★Self Catering

Quayside, The Quay, Waldringfield, IP12 4QZ

T:	+44 (0) 1473 736724
E:	donna.morgan@quaysidecottage.com
W:	quaysidecottage.com
Units:	1 • sleeps 2
Prices:	From £252-£476 per week
Open:	Year round
Description:	Stylish riverside cottage to suit couples. Set in grounds of owners' property, overlooking the beautiful River Deben.
Facilities:	General: ✿

WINGFIELD

Beech Farm Maltings   ★★★★ Self Catering

Beech Farm Maltings, Wingfield, Diss, Suffolk, IP21 5RG

T:	+44 (0) 1379 586630
E:	maltings.beechfarm@virgin.net
W:	beech-farm-maltings.co.uk
Units:	1 • sleeps 2
Prices:	From £195-£395 per week
Open:	Year round
Description:	Unusually spacious open plan first floor apartment on Norfolk/Suffolk border. Ideal base for exploration of coasts and Broads.
Facilities:	General: ✿

SHALFORD

The Laurels   ◆◆◆ Guest Accommodation

Dagden Road, Shalford, Guildford, Surrey, GU4 8DD

T:	+44 (0) 1483 565753
Bedrooms:	2 • sleeps 3
Prices:	Double and single: £23-£26 per person per night breakfast included
Open:	Year round
Description:	Secluded, comfortable detached house in a quiet cul-de-sac, near North Downs Way and Surrey cycle track. Good pubs very near.
Facilities:	Room: ⬛✕⬛⬛📺 ▢⬛⬛ General: ⬚⬛✕✿ Leisure: U⬛▶

BATTLE

A White Lodge B&B   ◆◆◆◆ Guest Accommodation

42 Hastings Road, Battle, East Sussex, TN33 0TE   SILVER AWARD

T:	+44 (0) 1424 772122
E:	janewhitelodge2@msn.com
W:	bedandbreakfastbattle.co.uk
Bedrooms:	2 • sleeps 4
Prices:	Double: £27.50-£30 per person per night breakfast included Debit/credit card accepted
Open:	Year round
Description:	Friendly family home, beautiful views, south-facing garden with outdoor heated pool. Ground floor en suite rooms. No smoking. Within walking distance of station, Battle Abbey, shops and on main bus route.
Facilities:	Room: ⬛✕ General: P✕✿ Leisure: ⬛U▶

CROSS IN HAND

Woodbine Farm ♦♦♦♦ Guest Accommodation
Cross in Hand, Heathfield, East Sussex, TN21 0QA

T:	+44 (0) 1435 867458
E:	poppyflower668@hotmail.com
W:	woodbine-farm.co.uk
Bedrooms:	2 • sleeps 4
Prices:	Double: £45-£56 per room per night breakfast included
Open:	Year round

Description: Traditional farmhouse with beamed bedrooms, four-poster bed and twin bedroom. At breakfast we use home baked bread, our own free range eggs and local produce. We can provide stabling and grazing for your horse! Peaceful location.

Facilities: Room:📺📺
General:✕✿
Leisure:Ʊ

EASTBOURNE

The Guesthouse East ♦♦♦♦ Guest Accommodation
13 Hartington Place, Eastbourne, East Sussex, BN21 3BS   SILVER AWARD

T:	+44 (0) 1323 722774
E:	fiona.bugler1@btinternet.com
W:	theguesthouseeastbourne.com
Bedrooms:	6 • sleeps 18
Prices:	Double: £30-£45 per person per night breakfast included Debit/credit card accepted
Open:	Year round

Description: Our property is decorated in contemporary style to a high standard, the renovation having completed in May 2005. We are the perfect choice for young families and anyone wanting flexibility, and stylish accommodation.

Facilities: Room:📖
General:✄

RYE

Four Seasons ♦♦♦♦ Guest Accommodation
96 Udimore Road, Rye, East Sussex, TN31 7DY   SILVER AWARD

T:	+44 (0) 1797 224305
Bedrooms:	3 • sleeps 6
Prices:	Double: £25-£30 per person per night breakfast included Euros accepted
Open:	Year round

Description: Spectacular views. Within walking distance of town centre. Own parking. All rooms have TV and hospitality tray. French spoken.

Facilities: Room:📖📺
General:✕✿

ST LEONARDS-ON-SEA

Beauport Park Hotel
★★★Hotel
SILVER AWARD

Battle Road, St Leonards-on-Sea, East Sussex, TN38 8EA

T:	+44 (0) 1424 851222
E:	reservations@beauportparkhotel.co.uk
W:	beauportparkhotel.co.uk
Bedrooms:	21 • sleeps 42
Prices:	Double: £130; Single: £95; both per room per night breakfast included • Debit/credit card, euros accepted
Open:	Year round
Description:	A late Georgian country house hotel set in 38 acres of formal gardens and parkland with its own heated swimming pool (Summer), tennis court, putting green, badminton and croquet lawns, French boules, outdoor chess and walks.

Facilities: Room: ✕📺♨🕯📻📺📡♿
General: 📖🎵❄📮
Leisure: 🎿🏊♒▶

ST LEONARDS-ON-SEA

Grand Hotel
◆◆◆Guest Accommodation

Grand Parade, St Leonards, St Leonards-on-Sea, East Sussex, TN38 0DD

T:	+44 (0) 4401 4244 28510
E:	petermann@grandhotelhastings.co.uk
W:	grandhotelhastings.co.uk
Bedrooms:	20 • sleeps 46
Prices:	Single: £15-£25 per person per night breakfast included Euros accepted
Open:	Year round
Description:	This well-established prime seafront hotel, just 0.5 miles from Hastings Pier and only 10 minutes' walk from Warrior Square railway station, welcomes everyone, including children. Unrestricted and disabled parking in front of hotel.

Facilities: Room: 📺♨📺
General: ✂📻✕📮

BIRDHAM

Croftside Cottage
★★★★B&B

Main Road, Birdham, Chichester, West Sussex, PO20 7HS

T:	+44 (0) 1243 512864
E:	info@croftside.com
W:	croftside.com
Bedrooms:	4 • sleeps 8
Prices:	Double: £32.50-£39.90; Single: £25-£39.90; both per person per night breakfast included • Euros accepted
Open:	Year round
Description:	Situated on the borders of the picturesque area of outstanding natural beauty that is Chichester Harbour. We invite you to spend some quality time with us at Croftside. Our aim is to afford you a warm welcome.

Facilities: Room: 📺
General: ✂P✕❄
Leisure: 🚲

CHICHESTER

Pen Cottage
♦♦♦ Guest Accommodation

The Drive, Summersdale, Chichester, West Sussex, PO19 5QA

T:	+44 (0) 1243 783667
E:	monicaandcolinkaye@talktalk.net
W:	visitsussex.org/pencottage
Bedrooms:	2 • sleeps 4
Prices:	Double: £28-£40 per person per night breakfast included Euros accepted
Open:	Year round
Description:	Well-maintained friendly, welcoming establishment in a quiet location. Close to the Festival Theatre, Hospital, University and Goodwood. A 20-minute walk to city centre.
Facilities:	General: ✿♨

EAST ASHLING

Englewood
★★★★ B&B

East Ashling, West Sussex, Chichester, West Sussex, PO18 9AS

T:	+44 (0) 1243 575407
E:	sjenglewood@btinternet.com
W:	smoothhound.co.uk/hotels/englewood.html
Bedrooms:	2 • sleeps 4
Prices:	Double: £26-£29 per person per night breakfast included
Open:	Year round
Description:	On B2178. Cottage-style bungalow. Pleasant garden, off-road parking. Between Downs and Bosham Harbour, close to Chichester, theatres, Goodwood, Fishbourne, Singleton and West Dean.
Facilities:	Room: ▥, General: P✿

LITTLEHAMPTON

YHA Littlehampton
★★★★ Hostel

63 Surrey Street, Littlehampton, West Sussex, BN17 5AW

T:	+44 (0) 1903 733177
E:	littlehampton@yha.org.uk
W:	yha.org.uk/hostel/hostelpages/866.html
Dormitories:	8 • sleeps 32
Prices:	Dormitory pricing: £15.50
Open:	Year round
Description:	This hostel is part of a redevelopment of Fisherman's Wharf on the east bank of the River Arun. Set in a traditional seaside resort just five minutes from the beach, it's a great base for all the family to explore the south coast, with family rooms throughout. The complex includes a cafeteria, as well as a tourist information centre.
Facilities:	General: ✄▥♨▣ ⌘

SHOREHAM-BY-SEA

Truleigh Hill YHA ★★★ Hostel

Tottington Barn, Truleigh Hill, Shoreham-by-Sea, West Sussex, BN43 5FB

T:	+44 (0) 1903 813419
E:	truleighhill@yha.org.uk
W:	yha.org.uk
Dormitories:	13 • sleeps 53
Prices:	Dormitory pricing: £9.95-£13.95 • Debit/credit card accepted
Open:	Year round except Christmas and New Year
Description:	Ideal base for family or group holidays in a well-appointed modern building on old barn site, high on the South Downs with superb views to the coast five miles away.
Facilities:	Room: ⬆✖ⅢⅢ,TV General: ✔P✄🚌✖🧺♨ Leisure: ♻

WARNINGCAMP

YHA Arundel ★★★★ Hostel

Warningcamp, Arundel, West Sussex, BN18 9QY

T:	+44 (0) 1903 882204
E:	arundel@yha.org.uk
W:	yha.org.uk/hostel/hostelpages/154.html
Dormitories:	14 • sleeps 62
Prices:	Dormitory pricing: £19.95
Open:	Year round
Description:	Enjoy the best of both worlds in this handsome Georgian mansion. At the end of a private road with a spacious front lawn, it's well away from the busy traffic of Arundel yet just over a mile from the town centre. There's walking aplenty – the Monarch's Way will lead you onto the South Downs or, for an evening stroll, follow the riverside path to Arundel.
Facilities:	Room: TV General: ✔P✖✱ Leisure: ♠

WEST MARDEN

The Old Stables, West Marden ★★★★★ Self Catering

West Marden Farm, West Marden, Chichester, West Sussex PO18 9ES

T:	+44 (0) 23 9263 1382
E:	carole.edney@btopenworld.com
W:	theoldstables.net
Units:	1 • sleeps 4
Prices:	From £300-£780 per week
Open:	Year round
Description:	A converted, single-storey beamed cottage, former stables. Fully furnished and equipped with two en suite bedrooms, offering accommodation for four people. Shared use of pool in high summer.
Facilities:	General: ⬆🧺 Leisure: ⚘

BAXTERLEY

Hipsley Farm Cottages ★★★★ Self Catering & Serviced

Hipsley Lane, Hurley, Atherstone, Warwickshire, CV9 2HS

T:	+44 (0) 1827 872437
E:	ann@hipsleyco.uk
W:	hipsley.co.uk
Bedrooms:	7 • sleeps 26
Prices:	From £295-£650 per week • Debit/credit card, euros accepted
Open:	Year round
Description:	Converted farm cottages in quiet countryside. Fully-equipped kitchens. Putting green and brick barbecue on site. Junction 10, M42/A5 three miles.
Facilities:	General: P🏠❄️ Leisure: ►

BROOM

Broom Hall Inn ♦♦♦ Guest Accommodation

Bidford Road, Broom, Alcester, Warwickshire, B50 4HE

T:	+44 (0) 1789 773757
Bedrooms:	12 • sleeps 20
Prices:	Double and single: £30 £35 per person per night breakfast included • Debit/credit card, cheques/cash accepted
Open:	Year round
Description:	Family-owned country inn with carvery restaurant and extensive range of bar meals. Close to Stratford-upon-Avon and Cotswolds.
Facilities:	Room: ✕◻️♿️🔲📺 General: 🍴✕❄️ Leisure: ∪🐴►

LONG COMPTON

Butlers Road Farm ♦♦♦ Guest Accommodation

Butlers Road Farm, Long Compton, Shipston-on-Stour, Warwickshire, CV36 5JZ

T:	+44 (0) 1608 684262
E:	eileenwhittaker@easicom.com
Bedrooms:	3 • sleeps 8
Prices:	Double: £45 per person per night breakfast included Cheques/cash accepted
Open:	Year round
Description:	Early 18thC Listed stone farmhouse on a happy working stock farm. Genial welcome, creature comforts, local pub within walking distance. Situated adjacent to A3400 between Oxford and Stratford-Upon-Avon. Open all year.
Facilities:	Room: 📺🕐 General: 🔌❄️ Leisure: ∪🚴🐴►

WARWICKSHIRE

RUGBY

Magnolia House ♦♦♦♦Guest Accommodation

82 Hillmorton Road, Rugby, Warwickshire, CV22 5AF

T:	+44 (0) 1788 542807
E:	info@magnoliahouserugby.com
W:	magnoliahouserugby.com
Bedrooms:	4 • sleeps 6
Prices:	Double: £44; Single: £30-£36; both per room per night breakfast included
Open:	Year round
Description:	Lovely guesthouse providing quality comforts. Ideal for short and long stay visitors, short walk to Rugby town and amenities.
Facilities:	Room: 🛏 General: ⚡P🔲

STRATFORD-UPON-AVON

Grosvenor Villa ★★★Guesthouse

9 Evesham Place, Stratford-upon-Avon, Warwickshire, CV37 6HT

T:	+44 (0) 1789 266192
E:	marion@grosvenorvilla.com
W:	grosvenorvilla.co.uk
Bedrooms:	7 • sleeps 14
Prices:	Double and single: £20-£26 per person per night breakfast included • Debit/credit card, cheques/cash accepted
Open:	Year round
Description:	Grosvenor Villa is an authentically restored Victorian family house. Ten minutes' walk from the town centre and theatre.
Facilities:	Room: 🍽📺📶 General: 🚗

WILTSHIRE

DINTON

Marshwood Farm B&B ★★★★B&B

Dinton, Salisbury, Wiltshire, SP3 5ET

T:	+44 (0) 1722 716334
E:	marshwood1@btconnect.com
W:	marshwoodfarm.co.uk
Bedrooms:	2 • sleeps 5
Prices:	Double: £25-£35 per person per night breakfast included
Open:	Year round
Description:	17thC farmhouse on working farm, warm welcome. Ideal for walking, cycling and touring.
Facilities:	Room: 🍽📺📶 General: ⚡ Leisure: 🎾

DONHEAD ST MARY

Cedar Lodge ♦♦♦ Guest Accommodation

5 Deweys Place, Donhead St Mary, Shaftesbury, Wiltshire, SP7 9LW

T:	+44 (0) 1747 829240
E:	cedarlodge@onetel.com
W:	cedarlodge.org.uk
Bedrooms:	3 • sleeps 6
Prices:	Double: £30 per person per night breakfast included
Open:	Year round
Description:	An energy efficient 'Eco' home; glorious views; comfortable beds; hearty breakfasts; walks from the door. A welcoming home from home.
Facilities:	Room: ⬛✕⬛⬛⬛📺⬛ General: ✕P⬛⬛

MARKET LAVINGTON

The Green Dragon ★★★ Inn

26-28 High Street, Market Lavington, Devizes, Wiltshire, SN10 4AG

T:	+44 (0) 1380 813235
E:	greendragonlavington@tiscali.co.uk
Bedrooms:	3 • sleeps 6
Prices:	Double: £25-£30 per person per night breakfast included Single: £22.50 per room per night breakfast included Debit/credit card accepted
Open:	Year round
Description:	Family-run public house, situated in the heart of the village; comfortable non-smoking rooms; good home-cooked food. Off-road parking.
Facilities:	Room: ⬛✕⬛⬛⬛📺⬛ General: P⬛⬛⬛✕⬛

WOODFALLS

Wich Hazel's Apartment ★★★★ Self Catering

Wich Hazel, Slab Lane, Salisbury, Wiltshire SP5 2NE

T:	+44 (0) 1725 511599
E:	anneveleigh@aol.com
W:	wichhazel.co.uk/
Units:	1 • sleeps 2
Prices:	From £190-£325 per week • Cheques/cash accepted
Open:	Year round
Description:	Luxury, self-contained apartment located in a quiet country lane on the edge of the New Forest, just for two.
Facilities:	General: ⬛ Leisure: U⬛⬛

ACTON BEAUCHAMP

Hidelow House Cottages   Self Catering rating applied for

Hidelow House, Acton Green, Worcester, WR6 5AH

T:	+44 (0) 1886 884547
E:	hwv@hidelow.co.uk
W:	hidelow.co.uk
Units:	6 • sleeps 25
Prices:	From £246 per week • Debit/credit card, euros accepted
Open:	Year round
Description:	Idyllic rural retreat. Quiet off the road location with stunning views. Recently converted 17th/18thC hop-kilns and tithe barn with ancient beams, log fires, four-poster beds. Assisted wheelchair users cottages. Home-cooked freezer meals.
Facilities:	Room: 🛏 General: P🅿✖🛎☼📶📠 Leisure: ∪♪►

BREDONS NORTON

Sheepfold   ♦♦♦Guest Accommodation

Manor Lane, Bredon's Norton, Nr. Tewkesbury, Worcestershire, GL20 7HB

T:	+44 (0) 1684 772398
Bedrooms:	2 • sleeps 4
Prices:	Double: £20-£25 per person per night breakfast included
Open:	Year round
Description:	Non-smoking family house in small country village under Bredon Hill.
Facilities:	Room: 📺 General: ✖☼

BROMSGROVE

Woodgate Manor Farm ★★★★Guest Accommodation

Woodgate Road, Woodgate, Bromsgrove, Worcestershire, B60 4HG

T:	+44 (0) 1527 821275
E:	info@woodgatemanorfarm.co.uk
W:	woodgatemanorfarm.co.uk
Bedrooms:	3 • sleeps 5
Prices:	Double: £60-£65; Single: £32-£35; both per room per night breakfast included • Debit/credit card, euros accepted
Open:	Year round
Description:	Fully refurbished Georgian farmhouse with modern en suite rooms. Rural setting, good walks, local pubs. Convenient for M5/M42.
Facilities:	Room: ✖🍽🛁📺☕ General: P🅿✖☼

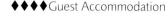

MALVERN

Orchid House   ♦♦♦♦ Guest Accommodation

19 St Wulstans Drive, Upper Welland, Malvern, Worcestershire, WR14 4JA

T:	+44 (0) 1684 568717
E:	sally@oml.demon.co.uk
W:	orchidmalvern.co.uk
Bedrooms:	2 • sleeps 4
Prices:	Double: £28-£32 per person per night breakfast included
Open:	Year round except Christmas and New Year
Description:	Modern spacious house. Views to the Malvern Hills. Convenient for the Three Counties showground.
Facilities:	Room: ✿✕🍳♿🛏📺🕸 General: P✿🚲

UPTON-UPON-SEVERN

The Orangery at Little Boynes   ★★★★ Self Catering

Little Boynes, Upper Hook Road, Upton-upon-Severn, Worcester, WR8 0SB

T:	+44 (0) 1684 594788
E:	info@little-boynes.co.uk
W:	little-boynes.co.uk
Units:	1 • sleeps 6
Prices:	From £225-£550 per week • Euros accepted
Open:	Year round
Description:	Quiet, cosy holiday base, equipped to high standard with access to indoor pool/spa. Near the Malverns, Cotswolds and Shakespeare Country.
Facilities:	Room: 🍳 General: P✕✿🖥 Leisure: ♪🕸

WYRE PIDDLE

Arbour House   ★★★★ B&B

Main Road, Wyre Piddle, Pershore, Worcestershire, WR10 2HU

T:	+44 (0) 1386 555833
E:	liz@arbour-house.com
W:	arbour-house.com
Bedrooms:	4 • sleeps 8
Prices:	Double: £60-£65 per room per night breakfast included
Open:	Year round
Description:	Fine Grade II Listed home in riverside village of Wyre Piddle, offering warm welcome, comfortable en suite bedrooms and excellent breakfasts.
Facilities:	Room: ✿✕🍳♿🛏📺🕸 General: P🚲

BEVERLEY

Number One
♦♦♦ Guest Accommodation

1 Woodlands, Beverley, HU17 8BT

T:	+44 (0) 1482 862752
E:	neilandsarah@mansle.karoo.co.uk
W:	beverley.net/accommodation/numberone
Bedrooms:	3 • sleeps 6
Prices:	Double: £25-£30 per person per night breakfast included
Open:	Year round except Christmas and New Year
Description:	Delightful Victorian house in quiet conservation area. Two minutes' walk from centre. Home cooking, library, open fires and lovely garden.
Facilities:	Room: ⬛✕⬛⬛⬛⬛, TV General: ✄⬛✕⬛⬛ Leisure: ⬛

DREWTON

Rudstone Walk
★★★★ Self Catering

Booking: Rudstone Walk Country Accommodation, Brough, HU15 2AH

T:	+44 (0) 1430 422230
E:	sylvia@rudstone-walk.co.uk
W:	rudstone-walk.co.uk
Units:	4 • sleeps 15
Prices:	From £330-£505 per week • Debit/credit card, euros accepted
Open:	Year round
Description:	Excellent cottage style apartments and B&B rooms with superb views of the Vale of York and Wolds. Central for touring East Yorkshire.
Facilities:	General: P⬛⬛⬛ Leisure: ▶

HOLMPTON

Elmtree Farm
♦♦♦ Guest Accommodation

Holmpton, Withernsea, HU19 2QR

T:	+44 (0) 1964 630957
E:	cft-mcox@supanet.com
Bedrooms:	3 • sleeps 5
Prices:	Double and single: £22-£25 per person per night breakfast included
Open:	Year round
Description:	Elmtree Farm is a Grade II Listed Georgian farmhouse B&B situated in Holmpton near Withernsea. It has retained many of its original features. The property is set in a quiet, picturesque coastal village.
Facilities:	Room: ⬛✕⬛⬛ General: ✄⬛⬛⬛ Leisure: U⬛♪▶

MARKET WEIGHTON

Towthorpe Grange ★★ B&B
Towthorpe Lane, Londesborough, York, YO43 3LB

T:	+44 (0) 1430 873814
E:	towthorpegrange@hotmail.com
Bedrooms:	3 • sleeps 6
Prices:	Double: £20 per person per night breakfast included
Open:	Year round except Christmas and New Year
Description:	Towthorpe Grange is a Victorian farmhouse built during the late 19th/early 20thC. It is the main house of a 300-acre farm originally developed as a hackney horse stud farm. It is on the Yorkshire Wolds Way.
Facilities:	Room: 📺 General: P✕

NORTH CLIFFE

Red House ★★★★ Guest Accommodation
North Cliffe, Market Weighton, York, YO43 4XB

T:	+44 (0) 1430 827652
Bedrooms:	3 • sleeps 6
Prices:	Double: £20-£40 per person per night breakfast included
Open:	Year round except Christmas and New Year
Description:	Comfortable Georgian country house with beams and antiques. Centrally located for Beverley, York and the Wolds. Warm welcome awaits you.
Facilities:	Room: 📺 General: P

PRESTON

Little Weghill Farm ♦♦♦♦ Guest Accommodation
Weghill Road, Hull, HU12 8SX — SILVER AWARD

T:	+44 (0) 1482 897650
E:	info@littleweghillfarm.co.uk
W:	littleweghillfarm.co.uk
Bedrooms:	1 • sleeps 2
Prices:	Double: £28-£30 per person per night breakfast included. Debit/credit card accepted
Open:	Year round
Description:	Set in open countryside, little Weghill is a traditional 18thC farmhouse, retaining many of its original characteristics. The house is surrounded by a large garden which is visited by a wide variety of birds, and bats in the summer.
Facilities:	Room: 📺 General: ✕ Leisure:

WELTON

Green Dragon Hotel ★★★★Inn

Cowgate, Brough, HU15 1NB

T:	+44 (0) 1482 666700
Bedrooms:	10 • sleeps 17
Prices:	Double: £49.50; Single: £40; both per room per night breakfast included
Open:	Year round
Description:	A 17thC inn on the Yorkshire Wolds. Situated in the centre of the picturesque conservation village of Welton.
Facilities:	Room: ✖📶🔥🍴🖼📺📶 General: ♈🚐✖🎵❄ Leisure: ♄

AIRTON

Beck and Brooklyn Cottages ★★★Self Catering

Settle Road, Skipton, North Yorkshire, BD23 4BD

T:	+44 (0) 1692 536662
Units:	2 • sleeps 9
Prices:	From £208-£543 per week
Open:	Year round
Description:	This pair of charming 16thC cottages is set in a quiet location just off the village green in Airton, in the heart of the southern dales. On the River Aire/Pennine Way, they offer lovely walks from the door to Malham Cove.
Facilities:	General: P❄🖼

BULMER

Grange Farm ◆◆◆◆Guest Accommodation

Castle Howard, Bulmer, York, North Yorkshire, YO60 7BN

T:	+44 (0) 1653 618376
E:	grangefarm3@yahoo.co.uk
W:	grangefarmbulmer.co.uk
Bedrooms:	4 • sleeps 7
Prices:	Double and single £24-£26 per person per night breakfast included
Open:	Year round except Christmas
Description:	A warm Yorkshire welcome to Grange Farm set in the beautiful Howardian hills-designated an area of outstanding natural beauty. Miles of open countryside and woodlands but only 14 miles from the historic city of York.
Facilities:	Room: ✖📶🔥🖼📶 General: ♨❄🖼 Leisure: ♄🎣

CASTLETON

Greystones   ◆◆◆ Guest Accommodation

30 High Street, Whitby, North Yorkshire, YO21 2DA

🕾	+44 (0) 1287 660744
E:	TheWedgwoods@aol.com
Bedrooms:	3 • sleeps 6
Prices:	Double: £21 per person per night breakfast included
Open:	Year round
Description:	Greystone is a typical stone-built Dales cottage. Centrally positioned in the village of Castleton. Close to local amenities. Secluded rear gardens, commanding views.
Facilities:	Room: ⿻✕🛢🚽 General: ✕♨️🎐

CLOUGHTON

Red Lion Inn   ◆◆◆◆ Guest Accommodation

28 High Street, Scarborough, North Yorkshire, YO13 0AE

T:	+44 (0) 1723 870702
W:	redlioninnscarborough.co.uk
Bedrooms:	4 • sleeps 7
Prices:	Double: £27.50-£30; Single: £25; both per person per night breakfast included
Open:	Year round except Christmas and New Year
Description:	The Red Lion Inn is family-run en suite accommodation, friendly atmosphere. In a beautiful country village adjacent to the National Park, Scarborough, Whitby railway line and Cleveland Way. Homemade food and cask ales.
Facilities:	Room: ⿻✕📺🛢🚽 General: ♨️✕🎵

CLOUGHTON

Standingstones Rigg   ◆◆◆ Guest Accommodation

Standingstones Rigg Farm, Whitby Road, Scarborough, North Yorkshire, YO13 0DX

T:	+44 (0) 1723 870984
Bedrooms:	2 • sleeps 5
Prices:	Double: £20-£25 per person per night breakfast included
Open:	Year round except Christmas and New Year
Description:	Eco-friendly farmhouse B&B, wind-powered electricity, beautiful views of land and sea, lovely garden, very peaceful.
Facilities:	Room: ⿻✕🛢🚽 General: ✕P♨️🎐 Leisure: ∪

EGTON BRIDGE

Broom House ◆◆◆◆ Guest Accommodation

Broom House, Whitby, North Yorkshire, YO21 1XD   SILVER AWARD

T:	+44 (0) 1947 895279
E:	mw@broom-house.co.uk
W:	egton-bridge.co.uk
Bedrooms:	6 • sleeps 12
Prices:	Double: £34.50-£39 per person per night breakfast included
Open:	Year round except Christmas and New Year
Description:	Broom House is a guesthouse establishment located in Egton Bridge. An excellent place to stay in all seasons at the heart of the Esk Valley. Egton Bridge is considered to be one of the prettiest villages in North Yorkshire.
Facilities:	Room: 🖼️ General: ✂️ Leisure:	

FILEY

Binton Guesthouse ★★★★ Guesthouse

25 West Avenue, York, North Yorkshire, YO14 9AX

₪	+44 (0) 1723 513753
E:	info@thislldo.co.uk
Bedrooms:	5 • sleeps 12
Prices:	Double: £25 per person per night breakfast included Debit/credit card accepted
Open:	Year round
Description:	Binton guesthouse is a friendly, four star establishment in the town centre of Filey and only five minutes' walk from the seafront and a 10-minute walk to Filey Golf Course, offering clean accommodation on a B&B basis.
Facilities:	Room: General: ✂️ Leisure:	

FRYUP

Furnace Farm ◆◆◆◆ Guest Accommodation

Fryup, York, North Yorkshire, YO21 2AP

T:	+44 (0) 1947 897271
E:	furnacefarm@hotmail.com
Bedrooms:	2 • sleeps 3
Prices:	Double: £20-£30; Single: £30; both per person per night breakfast included
Open:	Year round except Christmas and New Year
Description:	Furnace Farm is a small working farm, situated in the North York Moors. It is set in beautiful surroundings with magnificent views. It offers the perfect relaxing environment. The farm is a short distance from The Danby Moors Centre.
Facilities:	Room: General: ✂️ Leisure:	

149

GOATHLAND

Whitfield House Hotel ♦♦♦♦ Guest Accommodation

Darnholm, Goathland, York, North Yorkshire, YO22 5LA

T:	+44 (0) 1947 896215
E:	adriancaulder@btconnect.com
W:	whhotel.com
Bedrooms:	9 • sleeps 18
Prices:	Double: £66; Single: £33-43; both per room per night breakfast included
Open:	Year round except Christmas
Description:	A 17thC farmhouse providing modern comforts amid old world charm. Peaceful location. Cottage-style en suite bedrooms (non-smoking), with every amenity.
Facilities:	Room: ⬚✕⬚⬚⬚⬚⬚ General: ⬚⬚✕⬚⬚

GREAT AYTON

Susie D's B&B ★★★ Guest Accommodation

Crossways, 116 Newton Road, Middlesbrough, North Yorkshire, TS9 6DL

T:	+44 (0) 1642 724351
E:	susieD's@crossways26.fsnet.co.uk
W:	susieds.com
Bedrooms:	4 • sleeps 6
Prices:	Double: £22.50-£25; Single: £25; both per person per night breakfast included
Open:	Year round
Description:	Superb accommodation offered in a large detached house surrounded by 0.75 acres of beautiful gardens including large sun-soaked patio, where you can enjoy a relaxed breakfast on those warm summer days we always have in this country!
Facilities:	Room: ⬚✕⬚⬚⬚⬚ General: ✕⬚

GREAT LANGTON

Stanhow Bungalow ★★★★ Self Catering

Stanhow Farm, Northallerton, North Yorkshire, DL7 0TJ

T:	+44 (0) 1609 748614
E:	mary.stanhow@freenet.co.uk
Units:	1 • sleeps 6
Prices:	From £225-£535 per week
Open:	Year round
Description:	Stanhow bungalow is peaceful, relaxing and restful self catering establishment in Great Langton. Stanhow bungalow is detached, comfortable and well equipped within a private enclosed garden, including good parking and a garage.
Facilities:	Room: ⬚ General: P⬚ Leisure: ⬚⬚⬚

GRINTON

Grinton Lodge YHA ★★★★Hostel

Grinton Lodge YHA, Richmond, North Yorkshire, DL11 6HS

T:	+44 (0) 1748 884206
E:	grinton@yha.org.uk
W:	yha.org.uk
Dormitories:	16 • sleeps – Call for details
Prices:	Dormitory pricing: £16.30-£17.90
Open:	Year round
Description:	Grinton Lodge YHA is located in Grinton. This impressive former shooting lodge in the Yorkshire Dales National Park stands high on heather-clad grouse moors and commands spectacular views of Swaledale and Arkengarthdale.
Facilities:	Room: 📞🛁📺 General: P🚌🍴✕♻🅿 Leisure: 🚲🔍

HARROGATE

Brookfield House ◆◆◆◆Guest Accommodation

5 Alexandra Road, Harrogate, North Yorkshire, HG1 5JS   SILVER AWARD

T:	+44 (0) 1423 506646
E:	office@brookfieldhousehotel.co.uk
W:	brookfieldhousehotel.co.uk
Bedrooms:	7 • sleeps 14
Prices:	Double: £65-£75 per room per night breakfast included
Open:	Year round except Christmas and New Year
Description:	Brookfield House is a Victorian townhouse stylishly decorated in full original period features. The hotel is in a quiet tree-lined street within a short walk from Harrogate town centre and conference facilities.
Facilities:	Room: 🛁✕🖥🔌📞🛁🖥 General: ✕✿

HAWES

Hawes YHA ★★★Hostel

Lancaster Terrace, Hawes, North Yorkshire, DL8 3LQ

T:	+44 (0) 1969 667368
E:	hawes@yha.org.uk
W:	yha.org.uk
Dormitories:	12 • sleeps 108
Prices:	Dormitory pricing: £14.80 • Debit/credit card accepted
Open:	Year round
Description:	Hawes YHA is a great base for families, individuals and groups looking to explore the Yorkshire Dales National Park. It is ideally situated on the western edge of the market town of Hawes, (the home of Wensleydale Cheese).
Facilities:	Room: 📞🛁📺 General: ✕♻🅿🖥 Leisure: 🔍

HELMSLEY

Helmsley YHA ★★★Hostel

Carlton Lane, York, North Yorkshire, YO62 5HB

T:	+44 (0) 1439 770433
E:	helmsley@yha.org.uk
W:	yha.org.uk

Dormitories:	7 • sleeps 68
Prices:	Dormitory pricing: £16.30 • Debit/credit card accepted
Open:	Year round
Description:	Helmsley YHA is a popular newly refurbished hostel is in one of the prettiest country towns in North Yorkshire. A cosy, stone-walled building with comfortable, modern facilities on the edge of the National Park.

Facilities:	Room: ☎🛏📺
	General: P🚗✕🅿
	Leisure: ♻

HELMSLEY

Laskill Grange ♦♦♦♦Guest Accommodation

Easterside, Hawnby, York, North Yorkshire, YO62 5NB

T:	+44 (0) 1439 798268
E:	suesmith@laskillfarm.fsnet.co.uk
W:	laskillgrange.co.uk

Bedrooms:	6 • sleeps 11
Prices:	Double and single: £31-£37.50 per person per night breakfast included • Debit/credit card accepted
Open:	Year round except Christmas
Description:	Laskill Grange is a farmhouse located in Helmsley. Charming country house set in an acre walled garden, with lake, swan, ducks and peacocks. Emphasis placed on comfort, food, and value for money. Recommended on BBC *Holiday* programme.

Facilities:	Room: 🍴✕⬛🛏🔌📺🍵
	General: ♨🅿
	Leisure: ♻🎣⚓

INGLETON

Ingleborough View ★★★★Guesthouse

Main Street, Carnforth, North Yorkshire, LA6 3HH

T:	+44 (0) 1524 241523
E:	geoff@ingleboroughview.com
W:	ingleboroughview.com

Bedrooms:	6 • sleeps 14
Prices:	Double: £46-£65 per room per night breakfast included
Open:	Year round except Christmas
Description:	Ingleborough View is a small, family-run guesthouse in a stunning position in the Yorkshire Dales, where you can be sure of a warm welcome and a friendly atmosphere. The comfortable rooms are well equipped including TV and tea-/coffee-making facilities.

Facilities:	Room: ⬛🔌🛏📺🍵
	General: ✂P☀🅿
	Leisure: ▶

INGLETON

Ingleton YHA ★★★★Hostel

Greta Tower, Sammy Lane, Carnforth, North Yorkshire, LA6 3EG

T:	+44 (0) 1524 241444
W:	yha.org.uk
Dormitories:	14 • sleeps 91
Prices:	Dormitory pricing: £12-£14
Open:	Year round
Description:	An enlarged cottage set in the heart of the village with easy access to the Yorkshire Dales and Lake District.
Facilities:	Room: ☎🛏📺 General: P✕🧺♨ Leisure: ∪🍴

INGLETON

Rock Cottage ★★★★Guest Accommodation

Hawes Road, Carnforth, North Yorkshire, LA6 3AN

T:	+44 (0) 1524 241055
E:	info@rockcottageingleton.co.uk
W:	rockcottageingleton.co.uk/
Bedrooms:	3 • sleeps 6
Prices:	Double: £24-£25 per person per night breakfast included
Open:	Year round except Christmas and New Year
Description:	We offer quality, en suite accommodation. The house is built in traditional Yorkshire style with some beamed ceilings. It is warm and comfortable with full central heating, double glazing and additional welcoming open fires.
Facilities:	Room: ✕🛏 General: ✂P🛏🖳♫☀♨ Leisure: 🚲

INGLETON

Springfield Country Guesthouse ★★★ Guesthouse

26 Main Street, Carnforth, North Yorkshire, LA6 3HJ

T:	+44 (0) 1524 241280
W:	ingleton.co.uk
Bedrooms:	5 • sleeps 11
Prices:	Double: £26-£30 per person per night breakfast included Debit/credit card accepted
Open:	Year round except Christmas
Description:	Detached Victorian villa in its own small grounds with a fountain and conservatory. Car park and garden at the rear running down to River Greta. Ponds, waterfall and patios.
Facilities:	Room: ✕📺🛏📺 General: ✕☀♨ Leisure: ♪

INGLETON

Station Inn ★★★Inn

Ribblehead, Carnforth, North Yorkshire, LA6 3AS

T:	+44 (0) 1524 241274
E:	enquiries@thestationinn.net
W:	thestationinn.net
Bedrooms:	6 • sleeps 12
Prices:	Double: £27.50; Single: £30; both per person per night breakfast included • Debit/credit card accepted
Open:	Year round except Christmas
Description:	Public house, inn and restaurant in the heart of the Yorkshire Dales. Centre of the Three Peaks and North Yorkshire Dales National Park.
Facilities:	Room: ❄✆🏛🖵📺🗞 General: 🛗🚪🚌✕🎵❄ Leisure: 🔍

KELD

Keld YHA ★★★Hostel

Keld Lodge, Richmond, North Yorkshire, DL11 6LL

T:	+44 (0) 1748 886259
E:	keld@yha.org.uk
W:	yha.org.uk
Dormitories:	8 • sleeps 78
Prices:	Dormitory pricing: £14.80-£17.90 • Debit/credit card accepted
Open:	Year round except Christmas and New Year
Description:	Amid hills at the head of Swaledale sits the small village of Keld, its cottages clustered around a tiny square. The hostel, formerly a shooting lodge, stands overlooking the village.
Facilities:	Room: ✆🏛📺 General: 🚌✕🛗🗝

KIRKBY MALZEARD

Alma Cottage ★★★★Self Catering

Booking address: 12 St Stephen's Road, Cold Norton, CM3 6JE

T:	+44 (0) 1621 828576
E:	janet@lbarclay.demon.co.uk
W:	almacottage.co.uk
Units:	1 • sleeps 6
Prices:	From £260-£485 per week • Euros accepted
Open:	Year round
Description:	Comfortable three-bedroomed period cottage in stone terrace of quiet Nidderdale Village. Ideal for dales and moors, walking, cycling, riding, sightseeing and bird-watching.
Facilities:	General: P🏠🗝❄🖵 Leisure: ↻♪

KIRKBY-IN-CLEVELAND

Dromonby Grange Farm ★★★Farmhouse

Busby Lane, Kirkby-in-Cleveland, Middlesbrough, North Yorkshire, TS9 7AR

T:	+44 (0) 1642 712227
E:	jehugill@aol.com
Bedrooms:	3 • sleeps 6
Prices:	Double: £21 per person per night breakfast included
Open:	Year round except Christmas and New Year
Description:	Dromonby Grange Farm is a working dairy farm at the foot of the Cleveland Hills. Views of the moors from all windows. Very quiet and peaceful.
Facilities:	Room: 📶🍵🔌📺📺 General: ⚡PX☼🐾 Leisure: U♪

KIRKBYMOORSIDE

The Cornmill ◆◆◆◆Guest Accommodation

Kirkby Mills, York, North Yorkshire, YO62 6NP SILVER AWARD

T:	+44 (0) 1751 432000
E:	cornmill@kirbymills.demon.co.uk
W:	kirbymills.demon.co.uk
Bedrooms:	5 • sleeps 10
Prices:	Double: £35-£57.50 per person per night breakfast included Debit/credit card accepted
Open:	Year round
Description:	The Cornmill is a guesthouse establishment located in Kirbymoorside. Sympathetically converted 18thC watermill and Victorian farmhouse providing tranquil well-appointed B&B accommodation on the edge of North Yorkshire Moors.
Facilities:	Room: 📶🍵🔌📺📺 General: ⚡P♨X☼🐾 Leisure: U♨♪▶

LANGDALE END

South Moor Farm ◆◆◆Guest Accommodation

South Moor Farm, Scarborough, North Yorkshire, YO13 0LW

T:	+44 (0) 1751 460285
W:	southmoorfarm.co.uk
Bedrooms:	2 • sleeps 5
Prices:	Double: £23-£25 per person per night breakfast included
Open:	Year round
Description:	South Moor Farm is situated on the popular Dalby Forest Drive through Dalby Forest between Pickering and Scarborough. Accommodation comprises one double with windows facing south and east; one twin with window facing south and west.
Facilities:	Room: 📶🍵🔌📺 General: ⚡P♨X Leisure: U♨

155

LEYBURN

Eastfield Lodge ◆◆◆Guest Accommodation

1 St Matthews Terrace, Hawes, North Yorkshire, DL8 5EL

T:	+44 (0) 1969 623196
Bedrooms:	7 • sleeps 16
Prices:	Double: £27-£30 per room per night breakfast included
Open:	Year round except Christmas
Description:	Eastfield Lodge is a guesthouse establishment located in Leyburn. Family-run, private hotel offering large comfortable rooms with views over Wensleydale. Central for touring the dales and excellent for walking. All rooms are en suite.
Facilities:	Room: 🍵📞📺🛎 General: 🍽🚐☼🖤

LITTLE LANGTON

Hill House Farm Cottages ★★★★Self Catering

Hill House Farm, Northallerton, North Yorkshire, DL7 0PZ

T:	+44 (0) 1609 770643
E:	info@hillhousefarmcottages.com
W:	hillhousefarmcottages.com
Units:	4 • sleeps 12
Prices:	From £175-£440 per week • Debit/credit card accepted
Open:	Year round
Description:	Ideally situated between the Yorkshire Dales and North York Moors. Four well-equipped cottages converted from former farm buildings, retaining original beams.
Facilities:	General: P☼🖳 Leisure: ▶

LOW ROW

Birds Nest Cottages ★★★★Self Catering

Low Row, Richmond, North Yorkshire, DL11 6PP

T:	+44 (0) 1748 886858
E:	info@yorkshiredales-cottages.net
W:	yorkshiredales-cottages.net
Units:	2 • sleeps 5
Prices:	From £200-£350 per week
Open:	Year round
Description:	Birds Nest Cottages are self catering establishments located in Richmond. Renovated lead miners cottage with panoramic views over Swaledale. Lovely terrace with outside furniture for al fresco dining BBQ area shared with one other.
Facilities:	General: P☼🖳

MALHAM

Malham YHA ★★★Hostel

Malham YHA, Skipton, North Yorkshire, BD23 4DE

T:	+44 (0) 1729 830321
E:	malham@yha.org.uk
W:	yha.org.uk
Dormitories:	Call for details
Prices:	Dormitory pricing: £13.90-£17.90
Open:	Year round except Christmas
Description:	Purpose-built hostel designed by John Dower in one of the busiest walking centres in the Yorkshire Dales National Park.
Facilities:	Room: 📞🛏️📺 General: P✕🧺📶

MIDDLEHAM

Waterford House ★★★★★Guest Accommodation
GOLD AWARD

19 Kirkgate, Hawes, North Yorkshire, DL8 4PG

T:	+44 (0) 1969 622090
E:	info@waterfordhousehotel.co.uk
W:	waterfordhousehotel.co.uk
Bedrooms:	5 • sleeps 12
Prices:	Double: £85-£110 per room per night breakfast included Debit/credit card accepted
Open:	Year round
Description:	Delightful relaxed Georgian country house atmosphere. Sporting antiques, open fires, four-poster beds with superb cuisine and comprehensive wine list.
Facilities:	Room: 🛏️✕♿📶📺 General: ⚡✕❄️ Leisure: ∪

NEWTON-ON-RAWCLIFFE

Sunset Cottage ★★★★Self Catering

Booking address: Mrs Anderson's Country Cottages,
Boonhill Cottage, Pickering, YO18 8QF

T:	+44 (0) 1751 472172
E:	bookings@boonhill.co.uk
W:	boonhill.co.uk/sunset.htm
Units:	1 • sleeps 3
Prices:	From £195-£1,470 per week
Open:	Year round
Description:	With stunning views, this luxurious, wheel-chair friendly, bungalow is surrounded by fields in the North Yorkshire Moors National Park.
Facilities:	General: P🧺❄️ Leisure: ∪✎♪

NEWTON-ON-RAWCLIFFE

The Old Vicarage ♦♦♦♦♦ Guest Accommodation

The Old Vicarage, Toftly View, Pickering, North Yorkshire, YO18 8QD

T:	+44 (0) 1751 476126
E:	oldvic@toftlyview.co.uk
W:	toftlyview.co.uk
Bedrooms:	3 • sleeps 6
Prices:	Double: £28-£33 per person per night breakfast included Euros accepted
Open:	Year round except Christmas and New Year
Description:	The Old Vicarage at Toftly View offers stylish accommodation in a stunning location with wonderful south-facing views towards the Wolds. You will find a warm welcome and a high standard of comfort in a relaxing atmosphere.
Facilities:	Room: ✗⬛⬛♨⬛⬛⬛📺✎ General: ✁P⬛✗❄⬛

PATELEY BRIDGE

Edge Farm ★★★★ Self Catering

Booking address: The Croft, Heathy Avenue, HX2 9UP

T:	+44 (0) 1422 240829
E:	info@edgefarm.co.uk
W:	edgefarm.co.uk
Units:	1 • sleeps 12
Prices:	From £590-£1,450 per week
Open:	Year round
Description:	Edge Farm is a spacious five-bedroom detached property on the privately-owned Summerstone Estate, set in the remote and picturesque Upper Nidderdale Valley, a designated Area of Outstanding Natural Beauty. Area is popular with walkers.
Facilities:	General: P⬛♫❄⬛⬛ Leisure: ♪

PATELEY BRIDGE

Nidderdale Lodge Farm ♦♦♦ Guest Accommodation

Fellbeck, Harrogate, North Yorkshire, HG3 5DR

T:	+44 (0) 1423 711677
Bedrooms:	3 • sleeps 6
Prices:	Double: £25 per room per night breakfast included
Open:	Year round except Christmas and New Year
Description:	Spacious, stone bungalow. Beautiful walks and scenery in the Yorkshire Dales. Fountains Abbey nearby, also Herriot country.
Facilities:	Room: ✗⬛♨✆⬛✎ General: ❄⬛

PICKERING

17 Burgate ★★★★Guest Accommodation
17 Burgate, York, North Yorkshire, YO18 7AU   GOLD AWARD

T:	+44 (0) 1751 473463
E:	info@17burgate.co.uk
W:	17burgate.co.uk

Bedrooms: 5 • sleeps 10

Prices: Double: £85-£120 per room per night breakfast included
Debit/credit card, euros accepted

Open: Year round

Description: Opened 1 June 2005, awarded 5 Diamonds two months later. The only place to stay when visiting the delights of North Yorkshire. Luxury for the weary and stressed – indulge yourself.

Facilities: Room: 🕮🛏💻🖥
General: ✂🅿🍴☼🛂
Leisure: ♘🎣🏌🏃

PICKERING

Apricot Lodge ★★★★Guest Accommodation
25 Crossgate Lane, York, North Yorkshire, YO18 7EX   SILVER AWARD

T:	+44 (0) 1751 477744
E:	apricotlodge@beeb.net
W:	apricotlodge.com

Bedrooms: 3 • sleeps 6

Prices: Double: £30-£40 per person per night breakfast included
Debit/credit card accepted

Open: Year round except Christmas and New Year

Description: Apricot Lodge is a brand new B&B, opened February 2006. after all the rooms has been totally refurbished with your comfort in mind. We have been awarded five stars and a Silver Award.

Facilities: Room: 🕮🛏💻🖥
General: ✂🅿☼🛂
Leisure: ♘🎣🏌🏃

PICKERING

Bramwood Guesthouse ★★★★Guesthouse
19 Hall Garth, York, North Yorkshire, YO18 7AW   SILVER AWARD

T:	+44 (0) 1751 473446
E:	bramwood@fsbdial.co.uk
W:	bramwoodguesthouse.co.uk

Bedrooms: 6 • sleeps 11

Prices: Double: £25-£32; Single: £27-£32; both per person per night breakfast included • Debit/credit card accepted

Open: Year round

Description: Bramwood guesthouse is a Grade II Listed house dating from 1734, situated in historic Pickering, and is an ideal base for exploring the beautiful scenery of the North York Moors National Park.

Facilities: Room: 🛏💻📺🖥
General: ✂🅿🍴✗☼🛂

PICKERING

Karen's Cottages ★★★ Self Catering
83 Ruffa Lane, York, North Yorkshire, YO18 7HT

T:	+44 (0) 1751 473258
E:	hill@newmeadows.fsnet.co.uk
Units:	1 • sleeps 4
Prices:	From £200-£450 per week
Open:	Year round except Christmas and New Year
Description:	One-bedroomed accommodation with all amenities provided all on one level in large, secluded garden. Handy for moors and coast.
Facilities:	General: P✿▣

PICKERING

Loand House Court ★★★★ Self Catering
Cropton Lane, Pickering, North Yorkshire, YO18 8HF

T:	+44 (0) 1751 472587
E:	loandhousecourt@tiscali.co.uk
Units:	2 • sleeps 6
Prices:	From £240-£490 per week
Open:	Year round
Description:	Spacious luxury cottages with original features. Newly converted from traditional stone barns. Rural location. Panoramic views over Vale of Pickering.
Facilities:	General: P▣✿▣ Leisure: U♪►

RICHMOND

Frenchgate (66) ★★★★ Guest Accommodation
66 Frenchgate, Richmond, North Yorkshire, DL10 7AG

T:	+44 (0) 1748 823421
E:	info@66frenchgate.co.uk
W:	info@66frenchgate.co.uk
Bedrooms:	4 • sleeps 8
Prices:	Double: £32 per person per night breakfast included Euros accepted
Open:	Year round
Description:	We aim to provide excellent accommodation and food within the friendly and relaxing atmosphere of our beautiful 18thC home.
Facilities:	Room: ▣✕▣▣▦▣ General: ✕▩▦ Leisure: U♨♪►

RICHMOND

Restaurant on the Green ★★★ Guest Accommodation
5-7 Bridge Street, Richmond, North Yorkshire, DL10 4RW

T:	+44 (0) 1748 826229
E:	accom.bennett@talk21.com
W:	coast2coast.co.uk/restaurantonthegreen
Bedrooms:	2 • sleeps 4
Prices:	Double: £25 per person per night breakfast included Debit/credit card, euros accepted
Open:	Year round
Description:	Grade II Listed property with Georgian sundials, at the foot of the castle bluff. Near the town centre, the River Swale and countryside. Family-run guesthouse. Good food, fine wines. Good base for walking.
Facilities:	Room: ⌕✕⬜♨▥ TV General: ✕✕

RIPON

The Ship ★★ Inn
Bondgate, Ripon, North Yorkshire, HG4 1QE

T:	+44 (0) 1765 603254
Bedrooms:	4 • sleeps 9
Prices:	Double: £50 per person per night breakfast included
Open:	Year round
Description:	The Ship is a mock Tudor building in a residential area within easy reach of the city centre and ring road.
Facilities:	Room: ⬜♨ TV General: P⛾♨

ROSEDALE EAST

August Guesthouse ★★★ Guesthouse
3 Plane Trees, Rosedale, York, North Yorkshire, YO18 8RF

T:	+44 (0) 1751 417328
E:	mary@augustguesthouse.co.uk
W:	augustguesthouse.co.uk
Bedrooms:	3 • sleeps 6
Prices:	Double: £20-£25 per person per night breakfast included
Open:	Year round
Description:	August Guesthouse is a B&B located in Rosedale. It is situated in the heart of the North York Moors National Park one mile north of Rosedale Abbey. August House is ideally situated for walkers or sightseers.
Facilities:	Room: ⌕✕⬜♨▥⬚ General: P⛡☀♨ Leisure: ∪

SCARBOROUGH

Aartswood Guesthouse ★★Guesthouse

27-29 Trafalgar Square, York, North Yorkshire, YO12 7PZ

T:	+44 (0) 1723 360689
E:	aartswood@btconnect.com
W:	yorkshirecoast.co.uk/aartswood
Bedrooms:	13 • sleeps 26
Prices:	Single: £15-£20.50 per person per night breakfast included Debit/credit card accepted
Open:	Year round except Christmas
Description:	Our aim is to offer a friendly, informal environment for those wanting a pleasant break at affordable prices. All food is freshly prepared each day. We are on the north side of Scarborough.
Facilities:	Room: 🛏📺 General: 🍽🚗✕☀

SCARBOROUGH

Apartment 15 Easby Hall ★★★★Self Catering

Booking address: Bedwyn's Holiday Accommodation,
1 The Lodges, Filey Road, Filey, YO14 9PH

T:	+44 (0) 1723 516700
E:	info@bedwyns.co.uk
W:	bedwyns.co.uk
Units:	1 • sleeps 2
Prices:	From £190-£395 per week
Open:	Year round
Description:	Top quality apartment sleeping two-four guests. South Cliff Scarborough near esplanade. All mod cons. Recent conversion of old building.
Facilities:	General: P🍽

SCARBOROUGH

Atlanta Hotel ♦♦♦Guest Accommodation

62 Columbus Ravine, York, North Yorkshire, YO12 7QU

T:	+44 (0) 1723 360996
E:	atlanta62@aol.com
W:	atlanta-hotel.co.uk
Bedrooms:	7 • sleeps 15
Prices:	Double and single: £21-£25 per person per night breakfast included • Debit/credit card, euros accepted
Open:	Year round except Christmas
Description:	Atlanta Hotel is small, friendly hotel offering every comfort with good home cooking. Bedrooms are on two floors. All rooms have tea-/coffee-making facilities and TVs.
Facilities:	Room: ✕🛏📺 General: P✕☀ Leisure: �

SCARBOROUGH

Blands Cliff Lodge ★★★ Guest Accommodation

Blands Cliff Lodge, York, North Yorkshire, YO11 1NR

T:	+44 (0) 1723 351747
Bedrooms:	16 • sleeps 32
Prices:	Double and single: £21-£28.50 per person per night breakfast included • Debit/credit card accepted
Open:	Year round except New Year
Description:	Hotel within easy reach of the Futurist Theatre, the Spa Theatre, the beach and harbour. Shopping facilities and all other amenities.
Facilities:	Room: ♿📺 General: 🍽🚐✕🅿 Leisure: ⛳

SCARBOROUGH

Cavendish Hotel ♦♦♦♦ Guest Accommodation

53 Esplanade Road, York, North Yorkshire, YO11 2AT

T:	+44 (0) 1723 362108
E:	anne@cavendishscarborough.co.uk
W:	cavendishscarborough.co.uk
Bedrooms:	7 • sleeps 15
Prices:	Double and single: £28-£30 per person per night breakfast included
Open:	Year round
Description:	Small, family-run hotel, with a four diamond rating. Offering excellent home cooking, close to many amenities.
Facilities:	Room: ♿✕🖥♿📺🛜 General: 🚐✕✻🅿 Leisure: ⚲🚶

SCARBOROUGH

Hotel Phoenix ★★★ Guesthouse

8-9 Rutland Terrace, Queens Parade, York, North Yorkshire, YO12 7JB

T:	+44 (0) 1723 501150
E:	info@hotel-phoenix.co.uk
W:	hotel-phoenix.co.uk
Bedrooms:	14 • sleeps 37
Prices:	Double: £25-£33 per person per night breakfast included Debit/credit card, euros accepted
Open:	Year round except Christmas
Description:	Hotel Phoenix is a guesthouse establishment located in Scarborough. It set in a 15-roomed Victorian house, overlooking Scarborough's north bay and only minutes' walk from the beach, Scarborough Castle and other attractions.
Facilities:	Room: ♿🖥📺🛜 General: 🅿🍽🚐✕🅿 Leisure: ⚲🚶

SCARBOROUGH

Ramsdale Lodge ★★★★B&B

28 Grosvenor Road, York, North Yorkshire, YO11 2NA

T:	+44 (0) 1723 503964
Bedrooms:	1 • sleeps 2
Prices:	Double: £27.50 per person per night breakfast included
Open:	Year round except Christmas and New Year
Description:	Ramsdale Lodge is situated just a 10 minute walk from both the Scarborough South Bay beach and the town centre. Also the Esplanade where *The Royal* is filmed. We can offer a larger than average double room with en suite facilities.
Facilities:	Room: 🚿🛏️📺📶 General: ✂️❄️

SCARBOROUGH

Scarborough YHA ★★★Hostel

The White House, Burniston Road, York, North Yorkshire, YO13 0DA

T:	0870 770 6022
E:	scarborough@yha.org.uk
W:	yha.org.uk
Dormitories:	9 • sleeps 42
Prices:	Dormitory pricing: £13.90-£17.90
Open:	Year round except Christmas and New Year
Description:	Converted watermill in a streamside location on the outskirts of a popular seaside resort.
Facilities:	Room: 📞🛏️📺 General: P🚌✕🅿️📶

SCARBOROUGH

The Stuart House Hotel ★★★★Guest Accommodation

1 & 2 Rutland Terrace, Queens Parade, York, North Yorkshire, YO12 7JB

T:	+44 (0) 1723 373768
E:	h.graham@btconnect.com
W:	thestuarthousehotel.com
Bedrooms:	13 • sleeps 34
Prices:	Double and single £25 per person per night breakfast included
Open:	Year round
Description:	Friendly, family-run hotel, superbly situated overlooking North Bay and beach. Within 10 minute walk to main shopping centre.
Facilities:	Room: 🍳✕📭🚿🛏️📺 General: 🍽️🚌✕🅿️

SLINGSBY

Slingsby Hall   ★★★★ Guest Accommodation

Slingsby Hall, York, North Yorkshire, YO62 4AL

T:	+44 (0) 1653 628375
E:	info@slingsbyhall.co.uk
W:	slingsbyhall.co.uk
Bedrooms:	5 • sleeps 10
Prices:	Double: £30-£45 per person per night breakfast included
Open:	Year round except Christmas
Description:	Slingsby Hall is a B&B establishment. The Hall offers a warm, friendly and relaxed atmosphere for a peaceful and luxurious break in the North Yorkshire countryside. Set in five acres of stunning private grounds.
Facilities:	Room: ♥ General: ⚑🏠

STAINTONDALE

White Hall Farm Holiday Cottages   ★★★ Self Catering

White Hall Farm, Scarborough, North Yorkshire, YO13 0EY

T:	+44 (0) 1723 870234
E:	celia@white66.fsbusiness.co.uk
W:	whitehallcottages.co.uk
Units:	4 • sleeps 15
Prices:	From £165-£450 per week
Open:	Year round
Description:	White Hall Farm Cottages are located in Staintondale, 10 minutes from the Cleveland Way with stunning coastal and rural Views. Plenty of walks from the door including cliffs, woodland and streams.
Facilities:	General: P✽🖵 Leisure: 🚴

STAPE

Cropton Forest Lodge   ★★★★ Guest Accommodation

Stape, York, North Yorkshire, YO18 8HY

T:	+44 (0) 1751 471540
E:	croptonforestlodge@btopenworld.com
W:	croptonforestlodge.co.uk
Bedrooms:	6 • sleeps 12
Prices:	Double: £29.50-£35 per person per night breakfast included
Open:	Year round except Christmas and New Year
Description:	Cropton Forest Lodge is a B&B establishment in Pickering. In an enviable setting, surrounded by forest, wild flower meadow and open farmland in the North York Moors National Park.
Facilities:	Room: ♨✕🖳♥©🕮📺🖊 General: ✂P⚴✕♫✽🏠 Leisure: ∪🚴♪►

165

STAPE

Kale Pot Cottage ★★★★Self Catering

Kale Pot Hole, Newtondale, York, North Yorkshire, YO18 8HU

T:	+44 (0) 1751 476654
E:	mike@kalepothole.fsnet.co.uk
Units:	1 • sleeps 8
Prices:	From £275-£550 per week
Open:	Year round
Description:	Self catering cottage – 18thC – fully refurbished in secluded location in heart of North Yorkshire Moors, surrounded by forest and moors.
Facilities:	General: P🏠❄🖵 Leisure: ∪

SUTTON

Briar Cottage & Bramble Cottage ★★★Self Catering

Sutton-under-Whitestonecliffe, Thirsk, North Yorkshire, YO7 2QA

T:	+44 (0) 1845 597309
E:	jim.dickinson@btinternet.com
Units:	2 • sleeps 4
Prices:	From £250-£350 per week
Open:	Year round
Description:	Two unique one-bedroomed cottages situated at the base of Sutton Bank in the heart of Herriot Country. Natural water supply.
Facilities:	Call for details

SUTTON-ON-THE-FOREST

Goose Farm ◆◆◆◆Guest Accommodation

Goose Lane, York, North Yorkshire, YO61 1ET

T:	+44 (0) 1347 810577
E:	stay@goosefarm.fsnet.co.uk
W:	goosefarm.co.uk
Bedrooms:	3 • sleeps 6
Prices:	Double: £28-£32 per person per night breakfast included Debit/credit card accepted
Open:	Year round
Description:	Goose Farm is a B&B found six miles north of York in Sutton-on-the-Forest in open rolling countryside. The farm is on a quiet country road with a rural bus service at the door.
Facilities:	Room: ⤱✕🖳📶📺 General: ⤰P❄ Leisure: ♪

WETWANG

Life Hill Farm B&B

★★★★Farmhouse

Sledmere, York, North Yorkshire, YO25 3EY

GOLD AWARD

T:	+44 (0) 1377 236224
E:	info@lifehillfarm.co.uk
W:	lifehillfarm.co.uk
Bedrooms:	3 • sleeps 8
Prices:	Double: £30 per person per night breakfast included Debit/credit card, euros accepted
Open:	Year round
Description:	Set the counters to zero. Enjoy stunning views over the Wolds with rich variety of flora and fauna. Horses and dogs welcome.
Facilities:	Room: 🛝✕🖾🖐🔌🎞️🖐 General: ✂️🦺🐾🐴 Leisure: ∪🎾

WHITBY

Saxonville Hotel

★★★Hotel

Ladysmith Avenue, York, North Yorkshire, YO21 3HX

SILVER AWARD

T:	+44 (0) 1947 602631
E:	newtons@saxonville.co.uk
W:	saxonville.co.uk
Bedrooms:	Call for details
Prices:	Double: £113-£143; Single: £56.50-£86.50; both per room per night breakfast included • Debit/credit card accepted
Open:	Year round except Christmas and New Year
Description:	Owned and run by three generations of the Newton family since 1946, its close proximity to the North Yorkshire Moors and Captain Cook Country make Saxonville the ideal base for exploring the area on foot, by cycle or car.
Facilities:	Room: 🛝✕🖾🖐🔌🎞️📺🖐 General: ✂️🍽️🚗✕🖐

WHITBY

Wheeldale Hotel

★★★★Guesthouse

11 North Promenade, York, North Yorkshire, YO21 3JX

T:	+44 (0) 1947 602365
W:	wheeldale-hotel.co.uk
Bedrooms:	9 • sleeps 18
Prices:	Double: £34.50-£37.50 per person per night breakfast included Debit/credit card, euros accepted
Open:	Year round
Description:	Wheeldale Hotel is a townhouse hotel close to the North York Moors and film set of TV series *Heartbeat*. Premier, non-smoking, sea front hotel, in a quiet location on the west cliff, with magnificent sea views. Private parking available.
Facilities:	Room: 🖾🖐🔌🎞️🖐 General: ✂️🅿️🍽️🖐

YORK

Alcuin Lodge ★★★★ Guest Accommodation

15 Sycamore Place, Bootham, York, North Yorkshire, YO30 7DW

T:	+44 (0) 1904 632222
E:	info@alcuinlodge.com
W:	alcuinlodge.com
Bedrooms:	5 • sleeps 11
Prices:	Double: £58-£60 per room per night breakfast included
Open:	Year round except Christmas
Description:	Edwardian house in a quiet cul-de-sac. Bowling green opposite. Seven minutes walk to York Minster and all other attractions.
Facilities:	Room: ⬛✕⬥⛁. General: ✄

YORK

Bootham Gardens Guesthouse ★★★★ Guesthouse

47 Bootham Crescent, York, North Yorkshire, YO30 7AJ

T:	+44 (0) 1904 625911
E:	guesthouse@hotmail.co.uk
W:	bootham-gardens-guesthouse.co.uk
Bedrooms:	10 • sleeps 25
Prices:	Double and single £30-£35 per person per night breakfast included • Debit/credit card, euros accepted
Open:	Year round
Description:	Located only eight minutes' walk from York Minster yet are in a very quiet street with own off road parking for your private use. A purpose-built (January 2006) guesthouse that provides luxurious modern accommodation.
Facilities:	Room: ⬛⬥⛁,�📺🖳🖴 General: P✕☼♨ Leisure: ☍♦

YORK

Barn Hotel and Tea Rooms ★★★ Guest Accommodation

Hutton-le-Hole, York, YO62 6UA

T:	+44 (0) 1751 417311
Bedrooms:	6 • sleeps 12
Prices:	Double: £64-£76; Single: £32-38; both per person per night breakfast included
Open:	Year round
Description:	A warm welcome awaits you on the edge of North Yorkshire Moors at Barn Hotel. Small hotel and tea rooms run by local family. Home cooking with local produce, wherever possible, is a speciality. All rooms en suite and with beautiful views.
Facilities:	Call for details

YORK

YHA York International
★★★Hostel

Water End, York, North Yorkshire, YO30 6LP

T:	+44 (0) 1904 653147
E:	york@yha.org.uk
W:	yha.org.uk

Dormitories:	8 • sleeps up to 150
Prices:	Dormitory pricing: £13.50-£18.50
Open:	Year round
Description:	Well-established 150-bed hostel set in lush grounds and gardens. All just a short riverside stroll from the city centre. Rowntree family home.
Facilities:	Room: ♨✆🛏📺🕾 General: P🍴🚲🚌✕🎮🖥 Leisure: ♨🚲🔍

FOSTERHOUSES

The Fieldgate Centre
★★★B&B

Mill Field Road, Fishlake, Doncaster, DN7 5GH

T:	+44 (0) 1302 846293
E:	veggiehouse@ukf.net
W:	fieldgatecentre.org

Bedrooms:	2 • sleeps 4
Prices:	Double: £25-£32.50 per person per night breakfast included Euros accepted
Open:	Year round
Description:	Fieldgate B&B is five miles to the North of Doncaster on an organic small-holding amid beautiful, tranquil and ancient countryside. We are just over an hour's drive from the East coast, Yorkshire Dales and Peak District.
Facilities:	Room: ♨✆🛏📺🕾 General: ✂P⚡✕🌸🅿 Leisure: ∪🎣🏹

HAWORTH

Haworth YHA
★★★Hostel

Longlands Drive, Lees Lane, Keighley, BD22 8RT

T:	+44 (0) 1535 642234
E:	haworth@yha.org.uk
W:	yha.org.uk

Dormitories:	16 • sleeps 61
Prices:	Dormitory pricing: £12.80-£19.30
Open:	Year round except Christmas
Description:	Former mill owner's mansion built in the grand style, set in its own grounds overlooking the famous Brontë Village.
Facilities:	Room: ✆🛏📺 General: P🚌✕🅿🖥 Leisure: 🔍

HAWORTH

Rosebud Cottage ★★★★ Guest Accommodation
1 Belle Isle Road, Keighley, BD22 8QQ

T:	+44 (0) 1535 640321
E:	info@rosebudcottage.co.uk
W:	rosebudcottage.co.uk
Bedrooms:	5 • sleeps 10
Prices:	Double and single: £30-£40 per person per night breakfast included • Debit/credit card accepted
Open:	Year round except Christmas and New Year
Description:	A traditional Yorkshire stone cottage, deceptively spacious. All rooms have four poster beds.
Facilities:	Room: ⬛✕◱💧🚪🛏️📺⬚ General: ✕🚗✕☀️🛏️

HEPWORTH

Uppergate Farm ★★★★ Guest Accommodation
Uppergate, Hepworth, Huddersfield, HD9 1TG

T:	+44 (0) 1484 681369
E:	info@uppergatefarm.co.uk
W:	uppergatefarm.co.uk
Bedrooms:	3 • sleeps 7
Prices:	Double: £60 per room per night breakfast included Debit/credit card, euros accepted
Open:	Year round except Christmas and New Year
Description:	17thC farmhouse on a mixed working farm on the edge of Hepworth, a lovely Pennine village. Flag floors and exposed beams abound. Surrounded by beautiful countryside.
Facilities:	Room: ⬛✕◱💧🚪🛏️⬚ General: ✕P☀️🛏️ Leisure: U🚴

ILKLEY

Westwood Lodge Self Catering rating applied for
Westwood Drive, Ilkley, LS29 9JF

T:	+44 (0) 1943 433430
E:	welcome@westwoodlodge.co.uk
W:	westwoodlodge.co.uk
Units:	1 • sleeps 9
Prices:	From £325-£1,195 per week • Debit/credit card, euros accepted
Open:	Year round
Description:	Grand Victorian Listed house and adjoining cottages on the edge of Ilkley Moor. Quiet location, yet convenient for the town centre.
Facilities:	General: P🛏️✕☀️🔘⬚

TODMORDEN

Highstones Guesthouse ★★★ B&B
Rochdale Road, Todmorden, OL14 6TY

T:	+44 (0) 1706 816534
Bedrooms:	3 • sleeps 5
Prices:	Double and Single: £20 per person per night breakfast included
Open:	Year round except Christmas and New Year
Description:	Detached house set in 0.5 acres with lovely views over the open country, yet close to facilities.
Facilities:	Room: ⬜⬜ General: ⬜⬜⬜

TODMORDEN

Kilnhurst Old Hall ★★★★★ Guest Accommodation
Kilnhurst Lane, Todmorden, OL14 6AX · SILVER AWARD

T:	+44 (0) 1706 814289
E:	kilnhurst@aol.com
Bedrooms:	2 • sleeps 4
Prices:	Double: £35-£55 per person per night breakfast included
Open:	Year round except Christmas and New Year
Description:	A 16thC Grade II Listed property in a peaceful 10-acre setting. Our comfortable no-smoking accommodation has en suite bedrooms which enjoy excellent 21stC facilities yet retain the atmosphere of this historic hall.
Facilities:	Room: ⬜⬜⬜⬜⬜⬜ General: ⬜P⬜⬜⬜ Leisure: ⬜⬜⬜

TODMORDEN

Mankinholes YHA ★★★★ Hostel
Mankinholes YHA, Todmorden, OL14 6HR

T:	+44 (0) 1706 812340
E:	mankinholes@yha.org.uk
W:	yha.org.uk
Dormitories:	8 • sleeps 68
Prices:	Dormitory pricing: £9-£15.50 • Debit/credit card accepted
Open:	Year round
Description:	Mankinholes YHA is a hostel located in Mankinholes. An old manor house in a small, moorland village in the South Pennines.
Facilities:	Room: ⬜⬜ General: P⬜⬜⬜ Leisure: ⬜

TODMORDEN

Shoebroad Barn ★★★Self Catering

Booking: Pennine House, Pennine Grove, Todmorden, OL14 8AU

T:	+44 (0) 1706 817015
E:	thehorsfalls@beeb.net
Units:	1 • sleeps 8
Prices:	Call for details
Open:	Year round
Description:	Large, well contained barn in lovely open area with commanding views and only a mile from town centre.
Facilities:	Call for details

WADSWORTH

Hare & Hounds ◆◆◆◆Guest Accommodation

Billy Lane, Hebden Bridge, HX7 8TN

T:	+44 (0) 1422 842671
E:	info@hareandhounds.me.uk
W:	hareandhounds.me.uk
Bedrooms:	4 • sleeps 8
Prices:	Double: £40-£50 per room per night breakfast included Debit/credit card accepted
Open:	Year round
Description:	Country village pub with traditional hand-pulled beers. Open fires. Accommodation is in converted traditional barn.
Facilities:	Room: 🛁📞🛏️📺🔔 General: 🍺✕❄ Leisure: 🚲🏁